COMMANDERS IN FOCUS

ERWIN ROMMEL

KARL HOFFMANN

BRASSEY'S

Surveying his battle-zone. Erwin Rommel
preferred to visit all parts of the combat area
rather than just spend time with maps and
discussions at his headquarters.

First published in 2004 by Brassey's

An imprint of Chrysalis Books Group plc

Brassey's
The Chrysalis Building, Bramley Road,
London W10 6SP
www.chrysalisbooks.co.uk

Distributed in North America by:
Casemate Publishing, 2114 Darby Road,
Havertown, PA 19083, USA

Karl Hoffmann has asserted his moral right
to be identified as the author of this work.

British Library Cataloguing-in-Publication Data:
a catalogue record for this book is available
from the British Library

Library of Congress Cataloging in Publication Data
available

ISBN 1 85753 374 7

Photograph acknowledgements: Chrysalis Images.

Edited and designed by DAG Publications Ltd
Designed by David Gibbons
Edited by Michael Boxall
Cartography and layout by Anthony A. Evans

Printed in Singapore

CONTENTS

INTRODUCTION

To put a military commander 'in focus' – under the spotlight – some sixty years after his death, and in a different century from that in which he fought his wars, is not only somewhat unfair but also leaves anyone undertaking the task open to criticism and complaint. No manner or amount of research can enable a writer so distant from the battlefields, and thus unable to appreciate the personal pressures felt by the individual, truly to understand his subject and therefore produce an honourable and accurate account of his career. There is also the factor that many readers will already have an established opinion on the subject being studied.

This has always been the case, of course. Only the soldier who has actually performed an act of heroism or the officer who has issued a controversial order knows what drove the decision and then the reaction he felt. But this has not stopped generations of enthusiasts from studying the years of the Second World War, just as their predecessors had analysed earlier campaigns. The evaluation of the military commander is as avidly conducted as the scrutiny of politicians, sportsmen and entertainers, if not more so.

Although historians of his own land were slow to accept the fact, there can be no doubt that Erwin Rommel was a considerable performer in the Great War of 1914–18 and a colossal general in the Blitzkrieg and desert war battles of 1939–45. We shall acknowledge his weaknesses and errors – though we will surely find less in him than in many of his contemporaries – alongside his successes and talents because to do otherwise would be to demean the standing he achieved from modest beginnings and the hard work undertaken to reach the standards he did. But we shall certainly describe and assess all his substantial attributes.

There were many generals in the German Army who could have been better at their job than they were allowed to be, especially after the euphoria of Blitzkrieg had ebbed away and the reality of the Eastern Front and the huge Allied coalition in the west and south had dawned. Neither the Führer nor his army had planned for these reversals, and the formal rigidity and historic traditions of the German military hierarchy, having produced fine theorists, found too few of their number with the necessary initiative and enterprise. Innovation and dynamic action were hard to find while predictable and organised battlefield principles continued to be preached. Those who had the personal drive and imaginative thinking were quickly dragged down by inadequate tactical foresight and logistical planning at the top, and Erwin Rommel was most certainly one of these, though he had the strength to make the very best of what he was given to do. We shall consider what more he might have achieved, especially in the Western Desert, had he been given the resources that his generalship merited.

The oppressive and dictatorial nature of the Third Reich, where subservience and sycophancy were as likely to bring promotion as natural talent, dulled some fine men. Only a few broke the mould *and* kept their natural skills and, of these, perhaps Rommel was the finest example. If a true test of a man's achievement is the admiration afforded him by his enemies and competitors as well as his friends, then Erwin Rommel passes that examination. Seldom was Winston Churchill drawn to heap praise upon those who opposed his ambitions, but Britain's war leader wrote: 'His ardour and daring inflicted grievous disasters upon us, but he deserves the salute which I made him – and not without some reproaches from the public – in the House of Commons in January 1942, when I said of him, "we have a very daring and skilful opponent against us, and, may I say across the havoc of war, a great general".'[1] This quote by the leader of the nation that was in opposition to Rommel's country is more telling than any that have followed in the years since when military leaders and historians have lined up to heap retrospective praise on this man of modest physical stature, but a man-mountain on the battlefield.

This book will refrain from comparing him with those of other generations and eras, preferring to assess him alongside those he fought with and against. In comparison with the German military command of his time he was something of a maverick, though undoubtedly a brave one, and he surely confused the more reserved of his Allied enemies with his battlefield élan and energy. Keegan and Wheatcroft are of the view that 'Rommel possessed neither the innovative imagination of Guderian nor the large-scale operational mastery of von Manstein',[2] but did these men share all of Rommel's capabilities? Were they so capable of surprising hardened political and military superiors by the rate of their success, did they possess such an intuitive touch around a battle-zone, were they as inspirational to the ordinary soldier, possessing the common touch, and could either of them been a 'desert fox'? No, Erwin Rommel was not a von Manstein or a Guderian; he was Rommel and, in so many respects, a one-off.

As one might expect, the Rommel approach to command was not universally popular, even within his own armies. His constant urge to be at the front, and especially to change policy while he was there, did not sit easily with some senior staff officers. They could never be certain that their own orders might not be overridden during a Rommel visit, even when he himself had sent the instructions down the line only hours before! The more astute kept their counsel, recognising their chief's ability to make these changes for a purpose rather than simply on a whim, and this would be most obvious at the start of the Desert Campaign when strategies had to be evolved as faults were detected and improvements established. Here, after all, Rommel was on a steep learning curve like everyone else.

Churchill, with what might be seen as an element of jealousy, described him as a 'splendid military gambler', and while others might use the same description as a condemnation, believing that the battlefield is no place for idle risk, it is tempting to consider what Rommel might have achieved in the service of more even-minded masters. General Sir Claude Auchinleck, who fought him in the Western Desert, described Rommel as 'a master of improvisation',[3] but some would claim this skill only compensated for failings in the more formal processes of warfare and command. 'The Auk' was also to say that his opponent in North Africa was 'a general whose sole preoccupation was the destruction of the enemy'. But the Englishman, and other Allied officers, were constant in their opinion that Rommel conducted warfare with an honesty and a fairness not so common in many of his compatriots; it was another feature that distinguished this man.

Rommel wrote as well as he fought and we have benefited from his characteristically vivid but well-proven and accurate account of parts of his career. Remarkably, he chose not to embellish his descriptions but then perhaps he knew the plain truth was sufficient to mark his as a worthy soldiering life. Certainly he was aware of the high regard he enjoyed among the enemy, and of the fear that his name alone could induce within its ranks. He possessed a translation of Auchinleck's letter to 'All Commanders and Chiefs of Staff' that read: 'There exists a real danger that our friend Rommel is becoming a kind of magician or bogeyman to our troops, who are talking far too much about him. He is by no means a superman, though is undoubtedly very energetic and able … I wish you to dispel by all possible means the idea that Rommel represents something more than an ordinary German general.'

Even if it was correct for Auchinleck to issue such a note, one might argue with his choice of words. His men were seeing plenty of evidence that Rommel *was* more than simply 'an ordinary general'. Indeed, the German's methods of waging war saw few imitators in the British Army where commanders were seldom seen so close to the front as the German was likely to be.

Some reference works give minimal space to the man, and by so doing, betray their preferences or allegiances. Others tangle their reasoning when rating his military performance, trying to apply the same assessment to a backroom strategist and planner as they do to a campaign commander in the field, or a ruler of forces to a worker with them. Napoleon has to be judged by different criteria from Haig, as a Cromwell must to a Lawrence of Arabia, and a Patton or a MacArthur to an Eisenhower.

Martin Blumenson[4] suggests that Rommel was 'a throwback to the medieval knight in his personal traits', and that 'he had a touch for the grand occasion'. The latter comment is unfair, especially in respect of the early part of Rommel's career where the last thing on his mind in some of his successful minor and small force actions was that it should be 'grand'. But Blumenson is also ready to recognise that the man is 'increasingly regarded as a soldier who had a clear and compelling view of strategy and logistics'. The root of the man's soldiering ethic was to get the job done and, if necessary, placing himself where he could see it being done. An equally pertinent summation of his talents comes from Desmond

Young[5] who writes: 'From the moment that he first came under fire he stood out as the perfect fighting animal, cold, cunning, ruthless, untiring, quick of decision, incredibly brave.'

Erwin Johannes Eugen Rommel was a very special warrior, but, lest we fall into the same trap as others, not so unique that the pedestal we risk placing him upon suggests that he is impervious to criticism or should not have to justify standing above other masters of the military art. It was public recognition of his abilities by those who opposed him that accorded him his celebrity status and even created the sobriquet by which he will always be known – 'the Desert Fox'. He was a professional soldier with remarkable talent and a fine record of achievement, but he did have his failings, did make mistakes and could probably have inflicted even greater damage on the Allied war effort than he did. That he failed to do so was chiefly because of political decisions and unreasonable diktats beyond his control.

Field Marshal Erwin Rommel, seen here wearing his *Pour le Mérite* and *Knight's Cross with Oak Leaves.*

1

EARLY CAREER

War School

The records of Erwin Rommel's military life show that he joined the 124th Württemberg Infantry Regiment on 19 July 1910 and served with it for just over five years. It was not his first choice of career for he would have personally chosen to pursue his enthusiasm for the new science of aeronautics. As a child, having been born at noon on Sunday 15 November 1891 at Heidenheim, near Ulm in Württemberg, he had certainly shown considerable acumen in matters of design and technical detail (he built a glider with a friend, and it flew!) and would have welcomed the chance to join the staff of the Zeppelin works at Friedrichshaven. His father, however, discouraged him, perhaps considering that the everlasting military was a more secure path than the new flying machines, or maybe thinking back to his own days as a lieutenant in the artillery before turning to education; he told Erwin that he should join the Army. His decent education was not sufficient for immediate access to his preferred location, the Imperial Kriegschule at Danzig – the Prussian desire for the 'well bred' was still in force if in the process of erosion – and he was required to register with his local regiment as an officer cadet.

This was nothing more than a short pause in the career that would take young Erwin to the top because the rather weak and somewhat reticent child had blossomed during his teenage years. 'He suddenly woke up,' as Desmond Young[6] puts it, and had begun to show signs of the strong character that was to be his trait in adult life. Examinations had become easier, a fitness regime based around the sporting year gave him greater physical strength and the awareness of the team ethic and the value of a competitive edge enhanced his personal drive. What might have been had he been allowed to follow his first choice of career?

If there was to be no 'fast track' to officer status as was still common in young men of his age who came from the higher echelons of Prussian stock, the new officer cadet was not likely to let the fact slow him down. He was made a corporal in his third month and a sergeant by the end of the year, just five months after enlisting. Within a few more weeks he was at the Danzig Kriegschule, a small matter of nine months after those of superior breeding from his intake had arrived there without the need to work through the ranks. It is likely that the period actually helped Rommel to master the relationship he always enjoyed thereafter with the men who came to serve under him. Perhaps it is why he was content to fight at the front with the junior ranks, those with whom he had begun his military life. It may not, however, so obviously explain why he was later able to manage so ably those of more superior birth or better military connection when it might have been expected that their altered roles would induce the bearing of grudges.

At War School the young officer was said to be studious, because he had to be in order to master the tough curriculum, but most relaxed when required to show practical ability and a logical solution to military problems. Early in 1912 he passed his exams and returned to his regiment where he was eager to work with the new recruits.

There was still little indication that his was going to be a military career of such note. But for his own academic limitations he might have been seen as one likely to follow in his father's footsteps and become a behind-the-scenes teacher of military tactics and strategy rather than a practical hands-on leader for, at this point, he was an enthusiastic young officer but not demonstrably so in that he was content to be part of a team, usually in the background and not overtly sociable. Certainly he did not go out of his way to show personal ambition beyond that which a good work performance would achieve; he was slow to put himself forward and apparently found it unseemly to press his own virtues beyond those of his colleagues. This quiet, rather mundane and protected life was, however, to take a major turn when, on 1 August 1914, the regimental colonel announced mobilisation and, the following day, sent his men off to war.

It is difficult to believe that young officer Rommel was especially enthused at the announcement, though his later writings suggest that he and his colleagues were 'jubilant' at the news. He may have already been viewing 'live' warfare as an opportunity to employ his theories in practice, but surely this was to be a simple case of a man made by war. Psychologists have analysed Erwin Rommel, as they have many like him, and hypothesised on what talents the German took to war and what the conflict created afresh in him. At this point we have not quite reached the turning-point in Rommel's life and it can be argued that he set off for the Great War battlefields without firm aims and ambitions, at least on a personal level. Only when tested for the first time in the heat of battle did Erwin Rommel show the talents that later created the internationally heralded 'Desert Fox'.

First Live Action

Just three weeks after mobilisation Rommel was in a 'live war situation'. Patrolling on horseback in the early morning of 22 August, in thick fog and weakened by an attack of food poisoning,[7] Rommel reached the village of Bleid, on the Franco-Belgian border. He had been sent forward to assess the enemy strength and position, but very soon his platoon came under fire. Quickly assessing the situation as best he could in the poor visibility, Rommel took three men, by-passed the first farmhouse, from where the fire was coming, and moved close to another where he came across a group of enemy soldiers standing around as if the battle were many miles away. Without a second thought, and although he was outnumbered, he quickly opened fire, followed by his colleagues, and drove the surviving enemy into cover from where they returned fire. As the others from the platoon hurried forward in support, the team set about clearing the village, driving out the opposition with smoke from hay bales and breaking down doors with heavy logs, until it was safely under German control.

There are many military parallels where the first experience of fighting for one's life has brought about a change of character and added degrees of determination and purpose behind subsequent action. The same can happen in all areas of competitive life – the office clerk who, given the chance, becomes a super salesman, the reserve sportsman who blossoms when forced into the first team, and so on. For Erwin Rommel this was certainly stage one on his becoming a great battlefield commander – a minor skirmish in a long and tedious war perhaps, but an energising and uplifting experience where self-confidence received a major fillip. He had shown leadership, bravado and quick-wittedness; he had proved to himself and others that he could use these talents in the heat of war. Many fail this first test; Rommel passed it, and it was a life-changing event for him.

At this point the 1914–18 conflict was reasonably mobile, with the entrenched positions of the future yet to materialise. With his gastric problems still troubling him four weeks after this first success at Bleid, Rommel chose to take on three Frenchmen in a wood when completely alone and 'armed' only with an empty rifle. He was wounded in the thigh but again had shown courage and resolve in a non-standard situation and was recommended for the Iron Cross Class II. Just three months later, after convalescence, he was crawling with his men through a deep tract of French wire to get deep in the enemy positions. There he captured three houses and beat off the opposition who greatly outnumbered his troop, before withdrawing to his own lines with only modest losses. For this he was awarded the Iron Cross Class I; the name of Erwin Rommel was beginning to be noticed.

These actions were not the devil-may-care gambles of a glory seeker, but they do indicate a penchant for action rather than accepting the *status quo* and of setting an example rather than simply issuing orders. Perhaps Rommel was even surprising himself at this stage for these were hardly the actions of the somewhat shy, insignificant child or the modest, quiet officer cadet; no teacher or senior officer would have marked the adolescent Erwin as a likely expert in high-risk raiding and small-force warfare. They saw it now, however, and the military career of the man from Heidenheim was not far from making its first major upward turn. In the short term, however, he was somewhat demeaned when a lieutenant was given charge of his company. This required the recent recipient of his nation's premier military award to become a platoon commander again.

This slight was apparently taken with good grace and maybe he was given credit for that because, within months, he was promoted to first lieutenant and transferred to the newly formed Württemberg Mountain Battalion, operating from Münsingen under the command of a Major Sprösser. The work for which he was now to train would be far removed from the North African theatre he would later dominate, but it appeared that the Army had noted that this young Swabian was a man who got things done. His removal from the Western Front which thus avoided the static trench warfare has been described as 'good luck' by some historians but perhaps we should give credit where it is due. To Rommel for demonstrating his value in small force action, and to his superiors for finding a round hole for the round peg! It is true, of course, that if he had finished up in the dour trench battles he might not have survived, but on the other hand he might have shown the same innovation and bravery that he was to show much farther south.

The new unit was given a degree of autonomy that was not common in the German military. It was divided into battle groups whose constituents varied according to the task in hand and where its own commander was also given a freer rein than was normal. After training for more than a year the Battalion joined the Alpenkorps on the Roumanian Front with Rommel's Group quickly being given various tough and unconventional tasks. In the style of a 'Boys' Own' super hero, Rommel and selected small teams spent much time infiltrating enemy positions, usually by skirting the mountain top or valley strongholds by circuiting the upper slopes out of sight and sound to such positions. And these were not simply reconnaissance missions for the opportunity was never ignored to attack enemy patrols or defensive positions.

In August 1917 Rommel led four companies along a tortuous passage through woods around Mount Cosna, passing between two enemy posts just 150 yards apart without being seen and laying a telephone line as they went! Despite a serious injury to his arm, he continued to lead his men and was in the forefront of the attack that led to the capture of the fortified position. At Gagesti the following January he undertook a night raid – after sheltering with his men in the open in extremely low temperatures – that saw his small team capture 400 Roumanians whom he had caught asleep in their beds. These actions and others like them may not have been as grand or as celebrated as the work, some 25 years later, of Otto Skorzeny, seen by most as the originator of German Special Forces thinking. They did, however, clearly demonstrate that the Germans appreciated the value of specially trained, swiftly deployed special purposes forces long before such units were given specific and grandiose labels.

At the age of twenty-five Erwin Rommel was rapidly earning himself a reputation as a leader of courage and imagination who had long since overcome the slow start to his military career that his lack of privilege had brought about. His seniors were beginning to notice, even to seek his counsel and now he was to undertake his most dramatic action of the war, and do so with such success that his superiors would refuse to allow his talents to return to civilian life at the end of hostilities.

Rommel on the Italian Front

Now moved to Austrian Carinthia on the Italian Front, Rommel's detachment was called in with the Alpenkorps to help the Austro-Hungarian forces that had been suffering from Italian attacks in the Isonzo valley. Germany had not been active on the Italian Front until now, but the Treaty of Brest-Litovsk had taken Russia out of the war and thus released German units from the East. Fortunately for the ever-active Rommel, his region was one on which the increased German involvement would be centred. The Alpenkorps was to strike through the mountains and take three peaks – Mounts Stol, Matajur and Kolovrat. Rommel's team was to support a Bavarian regiment that was to lead the counter-attack, but he secured the agreement of his battalion commander, the same Major Sprösser with whom he had served at the outset of his war, to allow him to use some level of independent action. Once again moving at night, Rommel led his men to and through the Italian Front without being noticed with one unit capturing a battery in brief hand-to-hand fighting that saw only bayonets used and not one shot fired. The resulting gap was left guarded while Rommel returned to assist his first group that was under Italian attack and a swift drive into their rear saw this threat removed and more than 1,000 prisoners taken. Rommel's penchant for taking prisoners was to become legendary.

He was now given a further four companies to continue his progress. Locating a vacant road out of Italian view or control, he led his entire force in single file to a place on the road to Monte Matajur where it could intercept enemy troops and supplies heading for this strategic strongpoint. Soon he had captured 2,000 men of the 4 Bersaglieri Brigade and 50 officers plus a staff car and supplies of food. Using the car to reconnoitre, Rommel decided to move off the main roads and head for Matajur in a straight line. His heavily laden men marched for the rest of that day and the following night, and at dawn next day captured a further 1,500 men and officers of the Salerno Brigade by means of Rommel simply explaining the situation to them and demanding their surrender. Again, not a single shot was fired!

ITALIAN FRONT, 1917

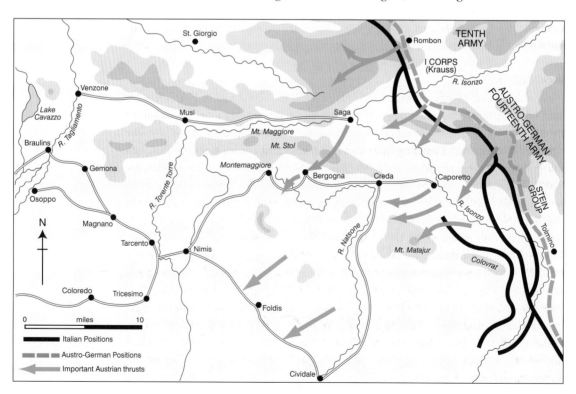

A little more than two days after starting his advance – when, remember, he was initially tasked with supporting another regiment – he reached the peak of the mountain and fired rockets to announce his achievement. He and his men had climbed 7,000 feet and captured 81 guns, 150 officers and more than 9,000 men; his detachment had lost just six dead and 30 wounded in the two and a half days. One can question the resolve of those he was fighting because the Italians seemed to surrender to him 'on request' and even carried him shoulder high on one occasion when his arrival stopped a debate between officers and men as to whether they should surrender when the Germans arrived. But Rommel was always ready to press for a result that preserved his men from combat and clearly, if he had outwitted the opposition, was very ready to demand their surrender.

This significant action truly established Rommel and was, lest we should think otherwise, entirely his battle, his talents and his success. As Lewin[8] puts it: 'It established him as a personality and, more importantly, it fixed his attitude towards the Italian Army.'

For this dramatic success Rommel was decorated with the *Pour le Mérite*, a remarkable achievement for one so young, and was promoted to Captain. It is likely his euphoria was short-lived however, for, after another daring night-time excursion through icy waters with a group of just six men during which the village of Longarone was captured, the young soldiering star was sent on leave. Furthermore, the offensive of which he had been part, and which could have taken the Austro-German forces far into the Po valley, was called off by High Command. Inexplicably, the new star of the German forces was given a staff appointment that he held until the war ended.

Between the Wars

One might expect that Rommel, of all military men, would have taken defeat in the war very badly, and been reluctant to return to non-combatant work in a military force denuded of power, influence and finance. In truth he, like others, had few options – he was not a wealthy man and had a wife and commitments – but, less commonly, this was a man who could sense some value in a time for contemplation and evaluation. The national loss hurt the man, but his future seemed more secure inside the remains of the Army than outside it, and he would use the immediate future to consider how the result could be different next time.

Rommel was retained by the Army in a rather modest post with the 124th Infantry Regiment where he worked diligently, if quietly, for two years before becoming a Company Commander in the 13th Infantry Regiment. Here he stayed until 1929 when he was sent as an Instructor to the Infantry School in Dresden where he used his personal time to pen *Infantry Attacks (Infanterie Greift An)*. This account of his experiences during the war and the tactics used would bring him to the attention of Adolf Hitler who was among the tens of thousands who acquired copies of the best-selling volume. Although the book certainly laid out all his achievements and experiences, it was not as much an exercise in self-promotion as it might have been. It was accurate, undemonstrative and informative and in this it represented the character of the man, especially the persona he showed when away from battlefield duty. Indeed, in these years between the wars, Erwin Rommel returned, to some degree, to the understated, somewhat reclusive character we see in his days before active service.

After a period as an instructor at the War College in Potsdam, Rommel was seconded to command Hitler's personal military security unit. This happened despite his various run-ins with groups and leaders of Hitler Youth who were reluctant to open themselves to the disciplinary and soldiering tuition Rommel had been asked to help with while at the College. There is no doubt that the Führer was instrumental in making the appointment, but for the recipient it was not the blessing it would have been for so many. Rommel had stoutly followed the Army tradition of remaining outside the whirlpool of politics and was not a supporter of the Nazi leader. As he would tell many people, he studied military theory, taught army students and fought battles for his country not for political ends or in support of so rigid an agenda. He did concede that he, like many of his countrymen that kept distant from the more controversial aims of the Third Reich, believed that Germany needed strong leadership to stave off the threat of Communism and rebuild the nation and, especially, the Army. The latter point was, of course, the reason why many of Rommel's colleagues and associates were drawn closer to the Führer even if others remained even more vehemently opposed than Rommel. The manner in which power in Germany was being centralised was not of direct or daily concern to many, including Rommel, and he, like his fellow Germans, did not realise the threat of the manic little Austrian until it was too late.

In his new role, the Swabian travelled with the Führer during the Munich crisis of September 1938 and the occupation of Prague a few months later. During this period of closeness to the national leader, Rommel came to form a view of the man who would eventually order his death. He was at times impressed with Hitler's good memory and his physical strength. He acknowledged that the leader could often find just the right phrase or statement to grasp the attention of those at a conference or a rally, questioning what power enabled an ordinary man, without great intellect, to suddenly become such a master orator. But he was never 'converted', never so swayed by the nearby mania to stop wanting to be a battlefield soldier.

Command of the Führer Begleit battalion was neither a taxing job nor an invigorating one for the wartime achiever. The position would have better fitted an overt Nazi rather than a fighting man, and the patronage potential will not have registered strongly with the Great War hero. Thus, when the Polish campaign was complete and Hitler, perhaps sensing Rommel's unease, asked the man what type of command he would be most happy with, he was told, 'a Panzer division'.

On 15 February 1940, Erwin Rommel was given command of 7th Panzer Division. He was forty-eight years of age and was about to implement Blitzkrieg.

2

BATTLE AND COMMAND

Rommel was not the only commander to apply the Blitzkrieg concept successfully, but he was particularly suited to its principles, being always happy when the action was fast and furious, bored and irritated if the situation became static. Quick-thinking and invigorated by commanding at the pace dictated by the strategy, he could also see every possible merit in a tactic based on these principles that still had impact against masses of the enemy and its equipment. He was not one who would be intimidated by the extent of ground over which he must fight, for he proved that he could forsake small force clandestine actions for air-supported heavy armour. Better than many of his contemporaries, he understood that military styles and methods had had to change down the years and were now facing more accelerated modernisation. He knew his special talents could bring 'added value' to this new technique. If his Germany was to achieve its aims in 1940 then the battles would be bigger than he had seen before, small-force actions would be the work of

On the receiving end of the Blitzkrieg. British troops pause at the roadside as Belgian civilians flee to the west.

someone else, and he would be implementing a new, awesome battlefield offensive that seemed to match every military tenet he held dear. He did not see the new strategy as one that would remove personal initiative from a military plan, but one that would enable him to demonstrate his leadership and individual talents on a grander scale.

It was undoubtedly to Rommel's benefit, and therefore also his nation's, that his experience of monotonous trench warfare during the Great War had been brief. The creed of fast movement that was to be the feature of Blitzkrieg was a hard lesson to learn for some of the veterans of those dire conditions, but Rommel was entirely happy with any development that would enable him to employ his favoured tactics with even greater pace and energy. His penchant for working at the front with his men was also ideally suited to the new tactic since, when it worked as intended, the divisional commander had to be more in touch with the spearhead than would be the case if slower progress were required.

The Swabian was destined to stay loyal to his tenet of staying at the front with his men. He contended that the higher the rank the greater the impact of a senior man sharing the dangers. He wrote that in the more testing moments of battle, when something special is required of the fighting man, a better reaction is obtained from an example being set or an order being given face to face than if the instruction is sent by radio from far behind the front.

Blitzkrieg was chiefly a creation of Heinz Guderian. It was an envelopment process whereby a breakthrough at the enemy's front was a crucial stage, but only the first, being quickly followed by flanking movements to strike at the side and then the rear of the opposing formation. It required initiative, and well-briefed and highly-trained troops, with close air support utilised to the full. Reconnaissance needed to be accurate and speedy based on armoured cars and radio communication, and the overall commander of a Blitzkrieg action was expected to be close to the front so that he could react to the fluid situation the tactic produced.

It should not be forgotten that effective logistics were also a crucial element of the strategy, as was surprise and pace. But even this counted for little unless Germany could find commanders capable of implementing a scheme that was the direct opposite to that on which most of their Great War veterans had cut their battlefield teeth. In Rommel they had a man who was 'made for Blitzkrieg'.

The Run into France
Rommel's 7th Panzer Division – it was to become known as the 'Ghost Division' for very good reasons – was part of XV Panzer Corps under General Hoth which, in turn, was a portion of Field Marshal von Kluge's fourteen-division Fourth Army. This made up the northern sector of von Rundstedt's Army Group A. Hoth's path forward in 1940 was to tackle the Meuse between Givet and Namur, having crossed the Belgian border through the Ardennes.

Rommel's Division left German soil at daybreak on 10 May and found its route mostly undefended save for craters and barricades left by the retreating

Belgians, who effected minimal resistance, and temporary attacks by a French tank formation operating with the Belgian defenders. By the second day, Rommel and his men were beyond Hotton and across the Ourthe, and by the third were at the Meuse; such was their pace that they were already far ahead of their sister divisions on either flank. Here we should pause to observe that time and again Rommel was able to move his units forward faster than his fellow commanders. Although we shall see that the speed was sometimes ill-judged because it prejudiced logistical support and planning, there is no doubt that this man had a very special talent to create pace on the battlefield.

Heinz Guderian is seen by most as having been the architect of the Blitzkrieg strategy.

Ludwig Beck, Chief of Staff in the pre-war years, had once told Rommel that the task of a divisional commander was to plan attacks using maps and telephoned communication and that there was no need to move from his divisional HQ.[9] It seems that particular conversation passed him by for it was not advice he ever took. It was normal for him to give his officers some freedom of action, but he was constant in his belief that they understood orders best when he gave them personally and that these officers and lower ranks could only benefit from seeing him at the front. His heartfelt opinion was that that was his place and while there he could fulfil all the traditional functions of his role and a good many more.

At the Meuse Rommel found many bridges destroyed and had to find other ways of getting across. Leading from the front as usual, he ensured that this happened by inspiring engineers and tank crews to take huge risks; at one point his closeness to the enemy saw him receive a shrapnel injury to his face.

Once across the Meuse and aware of the salient he was creating in the Allied front, Rommel began fully to deploy the Blitzkrieg tactics. At this point it was a

The withdrawing British troops had time to mine or destroy some bridges, as here in Louvain, but this did little to arrest the German advance.

risk he had to take for it could not be gauged what detrimental effects could befall his vanguard if it paused to wait for others and lose the advantages it had gained.

Now the full might of the Blitzkrieg strategy was seen. Even for the most experienced Allied troops, the impact of the Stuka dive-bombers was dramatic; they now had to look to the sky for the enemy as well as the horizon. What had been considered good shelter in the past – woods, buildings, etc. – was now just as dangerous as any other place. Even the most experienced infantryman was chilled to the bone when he heard the high-pitched scream of a Ju-87 and even the trusted refuges of hedgerows, trees, and barns seemed to offer scant protection now.

At times during its advance, the 7th Panzer Division averaged an incredible 35mph, so gaining an impetus that not only swept aside the opposition but continued to confound their compatriots. On the 16th von Kluge arrived at Rommel's Command Post to receive reports and discuss the plan to advance rapidly towards the Maginot Line defences. Rommel was aware of what he could achieve with the impetus he had already established, and von Kluge concurred, albeit with worries about the helter-skelter nature of the man.

Rommel was unstoppable now. Close-quarter fire-fights at the French defensive line did not delay onward progress towards Avesnes, Landrecies and Le Cateau, collecting vast numbers of surrendering Frenchmen as he went. After fierce tank battles around Le Cateau, 7th Panzer Division moved on the fifteen or so miles to Cambrai and took it with ease before pausing to regroup and plan ahead. At this point the Division was at the head of a 48km salient; too far for even its leader to continue without risk of over-extension or attack. During this rest period General Hoth arrived with the clear intention of stopping Rommel where he was so that other units could catch up and move forward again in greater unison. He cloaked his demand with the excuse that he was sure Rommel's men needed rest; the Swabian assured his superior that this current pause was all the recuperation his men would need, especially since 5th Panzer Division were about to arrive, having bridged the Sambre at Berlaimont. Unsurprisingly, the delay irked Rommel for, though he was a 'team player', he did not see why he should be held back simply because fellow officers were not showing his determination and resolve.

The Arras Débâcle

In a career that saw more triumphs than disasters, Rommel would no doubt have to accept that a low point was the strange panic that engulfed him after this characteristic burst across France. It was fleeting, but it *was* a command failure.

Deciding when to hold back a successful man is one of the most difficult tasks in man-management – in war or in peace, in soldiering or in commerce – and Hoth would not have expected a supine reply from his subordinate. Rommel made it clear that, having taken Cambrai, he wanted to move on, that he had the initiative with him and the battle-zone was brightened by moonlight.

Hoth gave way in the early hours of 20 May and the forward drive was recommenced, with Rommel no doubt doubly determined to succeed. But perhaps that was the problem in that his haste to prove his point led to his plans being incomplete or not fully thought through, and yet still full of pace. He might have claimed to have been distracted by Hoth's arrival at the front and his request for a further pause in his forward rush, but having rejected his superior's proposal and persuaded him to allow further advances, Rommel needed to continue to achieve. Perhaps he was too determined to succeed with Hoth looking on! But having taken Cambrai with comparative comfort he now came up against a British counter-attack at Arras.

The Ju-87 Stuka dive-bomber was a vital element of the Blitzkrieg strategy.

By daybreak on 20 May he had reached Beaurains, just two miles south of Arras, but his infantry had lagged behind the tanks and he had spent much of the night backtracking by armoured car to establish the reasons for this. He knew there were French and British forces in the area and he now found that French units had sought to break his line and needed to be dealt with before the main plan could be followed.

Having resolved this problem, and feeling he had regained the impetus, Rommel chose to move on north-westwards around Arras. The delays of the night and the pressures of the occasion seemed to make him unusually nervous about further attacks on his line of infantry following his tank-led advance so he deployed covering artillery and an armoured reconnaissance unit between the two. This only served to elongate the gaps rather than close them and again the commander had to undertake personal checks and directly lead the troops to where he wanted them to be. In this confused situation the formations came under attack from enemy tanks moving from Berneville and le Bac-du-Nord and the infantry was required to take up defensive positions as Rommel sought out some anti-tank guns to stop the enemy.

For once Rommel was not getting his own way. His anti-tank guns were facing the sturdy British Matilda Mk I and Mk II machines that were far too tough for the firepower he had at his disposal and he lost thirty tanks and armoured cars

FRANCE, 1940

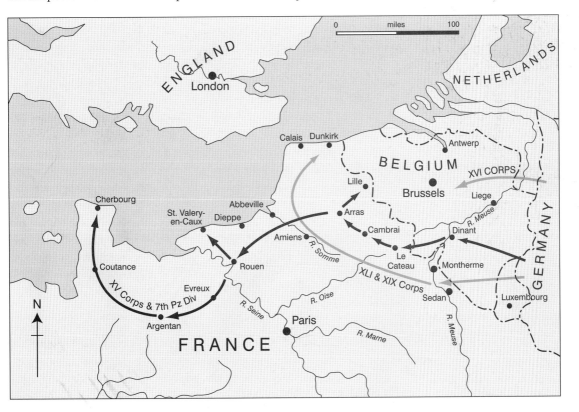

while accounting for just seven Matildas. In the mêlée Rommel is believed to have lost 89 killed – including his ADC, Joachim Most, as he stood alongside his commander, and 116 wounded and more than 170 missing. After such a smooth rampage into France this was a wretched shock to a man so used to battlefield success. He had not lost so many men in the entire journey from the homeland to this point. It was a sudden 'slap in the face' for a confident man. He had always been concerned about the men who fought under him and the thought that his impatience or, even worse, poor generalship might have led to the loss of so many hurt him badly. Certainly, had he allowed the halt that Hoth was pressing he would not have found himself so badly mauled on the slopes around Arras.

It was a particularly rude awakening. This was his first battlefield reverse, or more correctly, battlefield error, of any substance in an unsullied military career to this point. It was a note of caution but needed to be no more than that, and so it became to him. At worst, he acknowledged, it was a 'black mark' against him and maybe it sowed a few more doubts among those above him who had, until this point, given him firm or grudging support. For some it was a negative they would return to when considering him for other work; it had endorsed the view of some that Rommel could be hot-headed and impulsive, over-confident and imprudent. Whatever angst the man himself felt, we know now that it only strengthened his resolve and determination to do the job.

Göring clashed with Rommel on various occasions. His Luftwaffe failed to halt the British evacuation from Dunkirk when Rommel's tanks could have done so, and he made many promises of more aircraft for the Desert War but failed to deliver.

On to the Channel

It was typical of Rommel that he did not allow the happenings around Arras to bother him for long; after all, there was a job to be done and he was at the forefront of his superiors' planning. By 24 May the retreating British Expeditionary Force had been pursued to the low-lying ground around Dunkirk where everything began to stall again. Now it was Hitler causing the delay as he decided whether to risk his prized tanks on further action against the hapless British when he certainly needed the vehicles for the push on to Paris. The alternative was to heed the assurances of Göring who was adamant that his Luftwaffe could wipe out the enemy without recourse to time-consuming land action.

On the 26th, deciding to leave his panzers to do the job they were intended for, the Führer ordered Rommel to move on towards Lille. Despite temporary delays at the Canal de la Bassée, which saw the German again dashing hither and thither in the face of tough sniping fire to ensure the barrier was bridged, he maintained good pace even though he now had the armour of 5th Panzer Division also under command. Finding the French to have little stomach for the fight at this point, the commander started taking prisoners again, this time half the French First Army near Lomme.

Once again the impetus was with the energetic Swabian; he was using Blitzkrieg to startling effect. Where progress was blocked by destroyed bridges, he had engineers on hand; if a position had to be checked, fast motor-cycle teams were sent forward without delay. Even if he was not facing fierce defence, he still needed to have his wits about him and be ready to deploy all the assets he had at his disposal. Within ten days he was moving to cross the Somme and the Seine, and a week later was at the coast by St-Valery. Here he had four divisional Allied commanders and eight generals brought to him as prisoners and how he must have rejoiced when one of them told him, 'You were too rapid for us.' He now saw, as he described in a letter to his wife, that 'the war seems to be becoming a more or less peaceful occupation of the whole of France'.

In his final dash to his goal of Cherbourg, Rommel and his men covered 150 miles in a day, so completing a masterful demonstration of rapid, large-force advance that was, with the single exception of Arras, superbly managed from

Rommel is seen here with his regimental and Battalion Commanders after the Battle of St-Valery.

all points of view. Planning was diligent, logistics seldom found wanting despite the frenetic pace, and the commander the focal point of all that was good about this practical demonstration of the Blitzkrieg strategy. From the Ardennes to Brittany, Rommel secured more than 100,000 prisoners, over 300 guns, 450 tanks and armoured cars, and sundry other vehicles and equipment; he lost 42 tanks and less than 300 men killed, wounded or missing. The German forces had outmanoeuvred and destroyed the Allied formations set against them, and no-one had shown more determination and skill in the lightning advance than Erwin Rommel.

The Desert Fox is Born

The Germans had entered Paris on 14 June and within a month Hitler was ordering air raids on the British. By mid-September, with the Battle of Britain having been lost, the German leader was abandoning his ambitions to invade across the English Channel. Meanwhile, his partner in the attack on France, Benito Mussolini, had a force of some half a million men in Libya making moves towards Egypt where he confronted the 30,000 British troops. Despite the huge numerical advantage, the Italians achieved very little; General Richard O'Connor's conglomerate of British, Australian and Indian troops were to annihilate the Italian Tenth

THEATRE OF WAR FOR ROMMEL'S CAMPAIGNS IN NORTH AFRICA

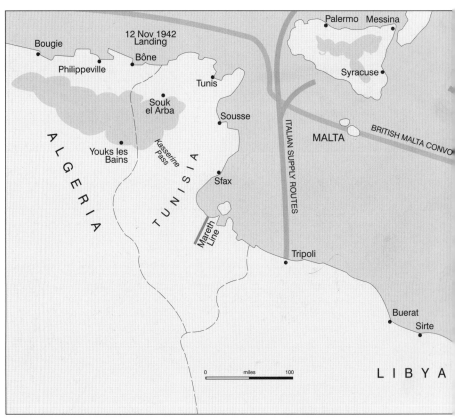

Army and force the enemy out of Cyrenaica. The Italian leader turned to Hitler for support; he wanted air power and troops.

Hitler was already looking towards Russia at this point, but he considered his alliance with Italy of sufficient importance to give some backing to Mussolini. If he could find the right man to lead a Division into this new theatre Germany could share more fully in the benefits that might accrue from a successful move in the Middle East. He might not be prepared to commit large numbers, but it was a venture that could bring rich rewards if successful. He sent some Luftwaffe units in January 1941 and called Erwin Rommel to a meeting at his Headquarters.

The Swabian, proven in the occupation of France, was interviewed first by Field Marshal von Brauchitsch and then by Hitler himself. The remit was to take a tank division and a light division to the new region and 'make a difference', although, in truth, the German High Command was already becoming so heavily committed to the Eastern drive that it saw North Africa as very much a secondary event. Von Brauchitsch and Franz Halder were among the Führer's advisers who were, in fact, urging Hitler not to send troops to Africa because of the known weakness of the Italians' fighting capabilities and the expectation that the British would be prepared to fight hard for control of the region. The

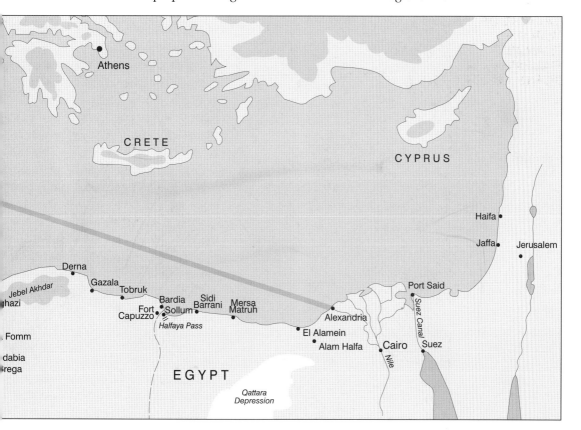

importance of the Mediterranean, Gibraltar and the Suez Canal won the day, however, despite the call of the campaign in the East.

While the proffered role was unforeseen – Rommel would have been expecting to be involved on the Eastern Front – it held some attractions. He would be master of his own area to a degree he had not enjoyed before, he would be able to set his own strategy and dictate tactics on a day-by-day basis. The down side was that he would be working in concert with the Italians of whom he had a very low opinion from his fighting *against* them in the previous war. He was not the first choice of his seniors for Major-General von Funck had been in North Africa since the turn of the year. Hitler had, however, become quickly disillusioned by his negativity; he needed someone with drive and determination, someone who would have an impact. Rommel was not a universal choice, for he was still not uniformly admired by his military seniors, Halder included, and because of this it can be considered whether his selection for Africa was only sanctioned because the appointment was perceived as a 'poisoned chalice'.

On 12 February 1941 Rommel landed in North Africa.

It will always be argued that Rommel would not have had such an impact in North Africa had he not arrived at a time when the Allies, recently so successful, were in such a state of self-inflicted disarray. In counter to this one is bound to say that the German had to begin working with Italian commanders and their forces who were in an even worse condition. They were under-performing on a grand scale, and his own formative force was inexperienced in desert warfare as too, of course, was their leader.

It can, though, be seen why the Swabian would have relished the challenge. The Eastern Front might, on the

Rommel poses for the camera in the middle of the main coastal road, the Via Balbia, in North Africa.

face of it, have been a bigger test and a larger war theatre, but this was the chance to have as near to sole control over a region as was possible in Hitler's armed forces. He had a chance to test Blitzkrieg in wholly different scenarios and across new terrain and, appealing to his national loyalties, represent his country on the African continent. Having said this, the initial edict was to prevent the complete loss of North Africa for the Italians; it was a defensive remit, not that Erwin Rommel was likely to view it that way for long.

On precisely the same day that Rommel arrived in Tripoli, Churchill's signal reached General Archibald Wavell, indicating that his dramatically successful army should now be divided between North Africa and the new threat posed by German ambitions in Greece and the Balkans. The latter theatre was to be given priority and the message stated that the best forces and equipment must now be concentrated on repelling German moves in this new region, assisting Greece and securing the support of Yugoslavia and Turkey.

At this point the British had taken Tobruk, Derna, Benghazi and El Agheila – all strategic possessions – and had captured 400 tanks, 1,300 guns and 130,000 Italian troops in their advance of more than 400 miles. They could have surely moved on to take Tripoli itself but the new instructions immediately deprived Wavell and Richard O'Connor of a corps. The fresh remits and responsibilities meant that they would be left with insufficient forces and inadequate command strength as the former attended to the new directive and the latter moved to take control of British forces in Egypt.

While the British were well aware of the German moves to bring a force to Africa, Rommel was ignorant of Hitler's plans for Greece. The British, however, thought they would have time to prepare to tackle the new arrivals because of the period they imagined would be needed for these troops to settle in, establish liaison with the bedraggled Italians and formulate policy. It was understandable thinking, based on their own tenets of troop movement and preparation practices; it did not, however, cater for the fact that Erwin Rommel would be performing the main role.

As soon as he landed in Tripoli, Rommel went into conference with the Italian commander, General Gariboldi and by mid-afternoon on the same day he was flying over the battle-zone in a Heinkel He-111 to familiarise himself with the terrain and its features. He had told the Italians that there were to be no more backward steps, that far greater use was to be made of air support, and that a whole-hearted defence of the Sirte region was essential, and that this was to be so even before the imminent arrival of German reinforcements.

It was so typical of the man that Rommel had 'hit the ground running' and was quick to impose his thinking on the Italian who was intended to be his superior. This instant disregard for formality and etiquette should have been expected because the German had a hatred of inactivity and prevarication. He would rather proceed at full pace with a general strategy he believed in than sit around refining it to a degree he considered was unnecessary. If the basic principles were right in the first place, and he was confident in his judgement in this regard, there was little reason for delay.

Not that Gariboldi had seen it this way. The Italian was far from enthused by the German's energetic approach to what his Axis partners had viewed as a very real setback against the British. Perhaps Gariboldi knew the standard of the fresh Italian troops arriving in Tripoli this very day! Rommel too was wary of these shortcomings because one of his first instructions was the construction of a host of dummy tanks that he hoped would fool British reconnaissance into thinking he had more tanks that he actually did and was even more active than he was. These fabrications of wood and blankets were mounted on German staff cars and driven to appropriate sites in the battle-zone.

At this point Rommel was expressing the view that the British would surely pause and re-set themselves if they saw some element of resistance ranged against them. He was right that the enemy would not pursue their recent advance, but it was not entirely for the reasons he thought.

With O'Connor now to be separated from his army that had routed the Italians, he recommended to Wavell that his replacement should be Lieutenant-General Philip Neame, VC. This man was undoubtedly a fine fighting soldier but he had no experience of desert fighting, was not a tank man, and had had no command of this sort before. Wavell, busy planning moves in Greece, agreed with O'Connor's proposal and in doing so probably felt the new man would have sufficient time to settle in before having to take any major decisions or action. Intelligence reports were certainly suggesting that neither the newly arriving

Italian captives in North Africa. Rommel found their performance mediocre, but was even more critical of their political masters.

Germans or the disorganised Italians would be in a position to mount counter-attacks in the near future.

The hasty and later to be shown ill-judged appointment of Neame, the removal of both O'Connor and Wavell from the region, and the loss of battle-hardened troops to another theatre, created problems enough for the British. but the Germans had not sent a traditional commander to spearhead their new venture. They had sent a man who did not conform to the conventional norm. Had Hitler chosen another commander for the formative Afrika Korps, that man might well have encamped in Tripoli, deferentially discussed tactics with the Italian nominated as his superior, made occasional visits to the North African terrain and ruminated long and hard on the options open to him. He would have then waited again while his newly arrived men quietly organised their machin-ery and supplies. But Rommel had completed most of these tasks in his first few hours! Given his dim view of the Italians' abilities, he was not going to waste time planning, especially with Gariboldi, when he knew what action was called for. 'I took the risk,' he was to say, 'against all orders and instructions because the opportunity seemed favourable.'

It seems that this energetic start met with the approval of Colonel Rudolf Schmundt, Hitler's Chief Adjutant, who had been sent out to Africa with Rommel so as to furnish the Führer with independent reports on progress in the theatre. When he returned to Germany, Schmundt wired back to Rommel that the actions he had taken in the first days had been fully reported to Hitler and well received. As a result, 15th Panzer Division would soon leave Germany for Africa and would travel with the Führer's own title for the formation – Deutsche Afrikakorps. This was the first reference to the name that would come to mean so much to the German people and their enemies.

Both in his haste and his disregard for the views of the Italians, Rommel con-tinued to ignore many general instructions. He would never disobey specific orders, but was skilled in the art of working on the edge of, and just beyond, recognised practices and official diktats in order to get the job done. Acting as a subordinate to Gariboldi was always likely to rankle with him, and keeping Italian and German forces separate was not going to serve his purpose in having an impact on the enemy. And it was not only the British who had expected the German to ease himself into his new environment; the German High Command had intended it to be the case as well, and any differences with the Italians could be resolved during such a period.

This policy was endorsed during a mid-March meeting with von Brauchitsch and Halder at Hitler's HQ that saw the opinion expressed to Rommel that the only offensive expected of him in the short term was to be an attempt on Benghazi. Furthermore, he was told he would receive no further troops for any-thing more ambitious. He rejected this proposal and insisted that by the Italians' own failures there it had been shown that Cyrenaica as a whole needed to be controlled if the possession of Benghazi was to be worthwhile.

Collective inefficiencies and Neame's lack of appropriate experience now combined with Rommel's energetic start and reluctance to accept the official remit to see a quick reversal of the positions in the desert. On 26 March Churchill signalled to Wavell his concern about German forward moves; Rommel, at this time, was unaware of the extent the British forces had been decimated by the withdrawal of troops for Greece, but was ready to make attacking moves anyway.

As early as 24 February, a small German unit had intercepted a British patrol, taking prisoners and destroying four vehicles, but by the end of March Rommel was in full attacking mode and within days Wavell would be accepting that some withdrawals and perhaps the sacrifice of Benghazi might be necessary. O'Connor was back in Egypt and Wavell, with other theatres now on his mind, was quickly losing faith in Neame, asking O'Connor to return from Egypt to replace him. This proposal caused further disruption, with O'Connor reluctant to undermine the position of the younger man he had sponsored so strongly, and now all three men were dragged into convoluted policy making.

If the British had acted more decisively at this point the whole of the war in North Africa might have taken a different turn. Without the quick success he was looking to achieve, Rommel's support back home might have evaporated rapidly. A British riposte would have certainly further weakened Italian enthusiasm, and Wavell's forces in the region, even if depleted, had both more experience and impetus on their side. An opportunity to defeat or stall the Germans was lost and instead of wresting the initiative from him, British inaction gave Rommel the confidence he needed to back his hunches yet further. If the British had simply showed that they were on the front rather than the back foot, their enemy might have employed more caution.

Rommel received more than 150 tanks when 5th Panzer Regiment arrived early in March, and by the 13th he had moved his Headquarters to Sirte. Shortly after that he sent out the first combined Axis force to protect against threats by the Free French around Murzuk, offering the German contingent their first long-distance desert march. The German continued to urge a better performance from the hapless Italians to the annoyance of Gariboldi who appealed for the re-establishment of the correct order of command. By now, however, the German High Command was beginning to share their commander's view of the Italian performance and thus ruled that their man was to take sole charge of the combined Axis forces in the region. This wise, if inevitable, decision compared well alongside the Allies' disorganisation where issues were being clouded and thinking becoming muddled by virtue of Wavell struggling to re-assess the situation on the ground, Neame finding himself out of his depth and O'Connor still eager to give the younger man his head.

Despite the modest reinforcements he had received and was promised, Rommel had been told by German High Command that he should not move beyond Benghazi in any forward drive he chose to undertake. His first target was, however, easily achieved when El Agheila was taken on 24 March, the main British contingent having drawn back to Mersa Brega. There was more of a battle for this important location when the Germans arrived there, but, with Rommel racing around the front-line of his advance and finally noticing an opportunity to outflank the opposition, it eventually fell, and a desperate British withdrawal left 80 trucks and gun carriers behind and the loss of six cruiser tanks.

On 2 April Rommel took Agedabia, just over 100 miles from Benghazi. He then divided his forces into three columns of which only one took the coastal route towards Benghazi, the others heading inland towards Msus and in the direction of Ben Gama. He had been surprised and somewhat confused by the poor quality of opposition he had encountered until now, but he was unaware that Wavell had told Neame that in the interest of keeping his forces intact, Benghazi should be sacrificed if necessary. If such a policy was stimulated by the knowledge the British had obtained from breaking German codes, namely that German High Command had forbidden a move beyond Benghazi, then Wavell and his superiors were underestimating their opponent.

But the British withdrawal was a haphazard, poorly organised affair, that only gave more cause for concern about Neame's abilities as a battlefield commander. Amid the confusion, command centres and the HQ of 2nd Armoured Division were deserted or destroyed by their occupants before Benghazi was left to the Germans. By April Rommel held the whole of Cyrenaica with the exception of

German infantry advance with caution towards Mersa Brega.

besieged Tobruk and was only held back from further expansive moves by the need for re-supply.

By 7 April the Axis forces were on the coastal plain at Gazala, nearly 200 miles beyond the point his political and military masters had told Rommel he should not attempt to reach before May.

Without involving himself in any significant direct action, but certainly threatening it, Rommel had quickly stamped his authority on North Africa. A new fighting animal had arrived there … a sly, determined hunter … a fox … a desert fox! Erwin Rommel admitted in a note to his wife that his superiors might not be immediately content with what he was doing but it would surely be applauded soon.

The Fox Moves On

Rommel was at the Egyptian border before his supply problem became too acute to continue. He had taken advantage of the British disarray, pushing at a door he found ajar and, sensing no resistance, had pushed on as far as he could. He had made Wavell and O'Connor, fine and proven battlefield commanders, appear weak and hesitant.

His frequent aerial reconnaissance had given Rommel an intimate knowledge of the terrain, and when the Italians claimed his planned routes of attack were suspect, the German was able to demonstrate that he knew better. Neame, far more reluctant to get forward with his men and new to the area, had no such awareness. Indeed, the British commanders were in dispute as to whether O'Connor should return to replace Neame, the former urging Wavell to accept the compromise of a short visit of support. But Wavell was under constant pressure from London, with Churchill for ever reminding him that with the men and equipment he was receiving, and despite losing many of his men to the Greek campaign, he could be expected to dominate the poorly supplied Germans and the inadequate fighting spirit of the Italians. If you could overrun a million square miles in East Africa, he was told, and kill or capture a quarter of a million Italians in the process, you can surely account for the forces the Axis powers range against you at present; he was a man living off the reputation of success in one campaign, a battle at which Erwin Rommel and his tough German soldiers had not been present.

At this point, to paraphrase Rommel, he was refusing to miss opportunities for the sake of trifles, whereas the British seemed hamstrung by them. Certainly Churchill was becoming as divisive in Whitehall circles as Adolf Hitler was prone to be with the upper echelons of the German military. Both men were mistrustful of much of the military theory put in front of them and each was more confident of their own 'gut reaction' than they should have been, but Churchill was, by necessity, a little more democratic and certainly more reasoned. The British war lord was as disillusioned by heavy military doctrine as was Hitler, and both men were led to some degree by outdated teachings and battle successes of historical heroes, but Churchill had a broader, more practical knowledge of modern military practice and his pressure for consideration of alternatives was more informed, his hard questions rooted in good sense rather than the mood of the day.

In many respects Churchill was as much Erwin Rommel's battlefield opponent as any set against him across the North African terrain. Despite his distance from the battle-zone, the British Prime Minister was very much in touch with the scene facing Wavell, O'Connor and Neame; he was seeing the same Intelligence reports, was aware of where each side had supplies *in situ* and *en route*, and was

The commander of the Australian 9th Division, Major-General Leslie Morshead.

capable of an almost photographic interpretation of the maps that were laid in front of him. While his diktats were not as final as Hitler's and he was more ready to acknowledge the attributes and achievements of his military chiefs in the field, Churchill's criticism when it came was usually more justified than an ill-informed rant from the Führer.

Rommel was employing Blitzkrieg in a different environment and against forces new to the phenomenon. The strategy forced those facing it to retreat, and this was accentuated when it was encountered for the first time. Neame and his officers had no answer; Rommel had the unfettered terrain of the desert to race across, finding it even easier than Belgium and France with their woods, valleys and rivers.

Buoyed by his success, Rommel wanted to move on and pursue the enemy across Egypt, aiming for the Suez Canal, though he realised that he must first take Tobruk; he couldn't think of crossing the border until his supply situation has been resolved. Churchill realised the strategic significance the fortified port was now taking on, and promised to send reinforcements to hold it. German High Command was at this point probably more supportive of their maverick commander than ever before, the prospect of capturing Suez being a most attractive proposition.

The Allies at last made the right moves and quickly. An Australian division was landed at Tobruk on 10 April and more troops arrived during the following 48 hours. Rommel realised he must attack the port without delay. The German personally directed the early moves, but, for the first time in this theatre, he met tough opposition. Within just a few days he moved from brash, confident director of advancing forces to a worried warrior unable to dent his opponents' defences. Not only was he getting no change out of Major-General Morshead and his Australians, equipped with tanks, anti-aircraft guns and uncommon determination within 'Fortress Tobruk', but the Egyptian border was being manned by groups of experienced harassing units under the command of Brigadier Gott. If his experiences at Arras had shaken his confidence temporarily, this sudden change of situation was bound to be a more severe test for Erwin Rommel.

Tobruk and Operation 'Battleaxe'

Rommel lost General von Prittwitz, who was to have commanded the newly arriving 15th Panzer Division, before he had even begun his work; he was mortally wounded by an anti-tank shell. He was also facing an enemy that was deter-

Tobruk was a strategic focal point in North Africa. Here part of the fortified port burns. When the port fell to the British in January 1941, 50 serviceable Italian medium tanks were captured. The picture shows two Italian M11/39 tanks put into service with the Australians – as denoted by the white kangaroos painted on the tank sides.

mined, did want to fight, and had the wherewithal to do so. But, early on, he continued to show typical energy and tried to employ tactics that were quicker in thought and deed than the opposition. But this time the enemy was not moving, it could not and did not want to.

This new phenomenon seemed to confuse Rommel. He dashed from one unit to another, stimulating initiatives though seldom waiting long enough to see whether they were working. In his rush he seemed to dissipate his forces rather than concentrate them on a possible weak point or two. Here we get the impression that Rommel attempted his tried and tested policies for too long before he understood that they were not what were required. For all his attempts to get his teams working more positively by hurrying to their positions and urging them on, perhaps this was one time when he should have sat quietly behind the lines, looked at his maps, studied his Intelligence reports and even thought back to his war college theories.

To be fair, he was short of adequate Intelligence reports that might have pointed him to an alternative strategy. He did not have clear maps of the make-up of the Tobruk defences until 19 April, though Italian High Command could have provided them earlier, and Rommel might have pursued this source more vigorously! Furthermore, it was not just the commander who was new to raiding such a fortification, his men had never been faced with a similar situation and certainly looked to an increasingly frustrated leader for guidance.

Within the Tobruk fortifications, Morshead had six infantry brigades, four artillery regiments, two anti-tank regiments, 75 anti-aircraft guns and 45 tanks and, above all, he had confidence that this was enough. His German adversary would not capture this vital stronghold by means of Blitzkrieg tactics, of rush and personal visits to the front-line forces; he would need to sit and conduct whatever siege he could manage and there was nothing in Rommel's past to suggest that this was a strategy he would be at home with.

By early March the German had come to the conclusion that he could not take Tobruk. His men were exhausted from the many futile attempts that had been made. and the new division and equipment *en route* would be unlikely to make a difference. As his confidence ebbed so the opinions of his superiors in German High Command altered, for some of the seniors there had been waiting for such a reversal. Questions were again being asked as to whether German forces should be in North Africa at all and, if they had to be, should they be commanded by a man whose unorthodoxy had only brought short-term gains. The very energy that had brought Rommel success in Europe, and initially in the desert, was now being highlighted as evidence of inadequacy. What the likes of Halder wanted was a more typical formal warrior such as himself!

There is no doubt that Tobruk was a rude awakening for the 'Desert Fox'. Rommel was never comfortable with losing troops to death or capture, and his tough demands on his men were as much for their own safety in a correctly executed manoeuvre. His own writings talk of how losses increased once he became involved in the static siege-style warfare at Tobruk and how the outcome of such combat was the destruction of manpower – the invaders – more than *matériel*.

Berlin sent General Friedrich Paulus, another veteran of the Alpenkorps in the First World War and, ironically, the man who would surrender Stalingrad later in the war, to evaluate the situation. His assessment was entirely logical – too few men, too little equipment, no chance of effective re-supply across the Mediterranean and a commander who was tactically inadequate; it was a report that was intercepted by the Allies and caused some relief to Churchill. Given the negativity he read into the German signals, he sought the opinion of Wavell only to get a reply that indicated the latter would now be prepared to move on to the offensive against Rommel if and when the imminent *Tiger* convoy of tanks got through. This reservation, though surely merited given that some of the tanks were destined for Crete and that all possible firepower of this sort was needed to combat the German strength effectively, would bring about the removal of Archibald Wavell from Africa far more quickly than Erwin Rommel could have managed. Churchill, however unjust his stance, was fast becoming incensed by his man's caution.

Against a need of some 50,000 tons of supplies each month, the Axis forces were receiving an average of less than 30,000 and with Malta such a remarkably dominating presence in convoyed supplies across and through the Mediterranean, the capture of Tobruk was the most likely event that might alter this dire situation. The retention of the port was vital to the Allies, its capture seemingly essential to a continuing and expanding effort by the Germans and Italians. Not for nothing was Churchill's comment as stark as it was – Tobruk should be held to the death without thought of retirement.

Churchill's account of this period in his own memoirs indicates just how depressed he was by the state of the war in the desert. His view of that theatre was perhaps one-dimensional and not based on first-hand knowledge, but he recognised a threat when he saw one, and Erwin Rommel was just that. From his perspective everything was going wrong, with the German involvement there disconcerting in its fact and dangerous in its potential. He cast Wavell as the villain and Rommel as the main danger. 'A new figure sprang upon the world,' he wrote after the war, indicating why he was pressing so hard for effective action against the man.

Before the end of May Wavell had his tanks, but Rommel also had 15th Panzer Division and soon had inflicted a defeat around the Halfaya Pass to hasten the former's departure, removed by Churchill. Operation 'Battleaxe', Wavell's parting shot, was already in place and launched by him on 15 June. The German, however, had 15th Panzer securing the coastal route at Sollum and Capuzzo and 5th Light Division covering his right flank. Even though he lost Capuzzo, he was able to allow the British to so spend their energies and ammunition on thrusts that would leave them open to successful counters as and when he chose to make them. By noon on the 17th signals were being sent announcing that 'Battleaxe' had failed and Churchill, who had placed such store by a whole-hearted attack on the Swabian upstart, was sent tumbling into another black mood. For his part, Rommel was visiting his successful troops and sharing in the joy of their achievement.

New Enemy, Same Ambitions

It was not lost on Churchill, who was to refer later to Rommel having 'torn the new-worn laurels from Wavell's brow,' that this was not an ideal time to introduce new leadership in the desert, but he was also of the view that it was so for both sides. He reasoned that the new Allied commander, Claude Auchinleck, might get time to settle in while his opponent did some research in order to detect any change of policy. The new man was made well aware that the *status quo* was not acceptable and that his German equivalent must be shown that North Africa was not his to conquer. Had London thought that the Germans' defeat of 'Battleaxe' would spur extended Axis activity there they would have been wrong for Hitler was becoming ever more focused on the Eastern Front and impervious to any representations that urged greater resources being sent to distant Africa.

It is clear that some thought was being given to the prize of the Suez Canal and the means by which such ambition could be realised, but these were themes for the planners to examine, not topics of signals to Rommel. No one was asking him 'what do you require to reach and control Egypt and the Gulf?' because their priorities were elsewhere. Some early successes in the East were encouraging, some thought that expansion down and around the eastern Mediterranean area might be possible at a later date, and thus it was in German interest to hold on to North Africa but without too great a commitment there. For his part, Rommel was thinking of reaching the Canal by the following Spring and Iraq thereafter, thus providing just such a strategic link to the Eastern operations by stopping the oil routing to the Russians from the south. But, in modern parlance this was 'blue sky thinking' and quite impossible unless German High Command performed a complete *volte-face*.

So Rommel and his superiors had to be content with planning how he could remain in control of the North African situation without significant reinforcements, while London seemed likely to send more men and equipment. He continually urged a move against Malta in order to improve his supply route and damage the British channels; he also realised that without this he could devise nothing more grand than containment and minor offensives. Some supplies did get through, but the coming months would see nearly fifty German vessels lost on the Mediterranean run.

The British hold on Malta was hugely damaging to the Axis forces in the desert. For remarkable little investment in terms of naval firepower, the British were exerting huge influence over the shipping from Italian ports. The Allies were also so much stronger in the air, with Axis supplies often being destroyed in the Italian ports and then, if they made it across the water, attacked in Benghazi and Tripoli, or the depots at Derna. Indeed, Auchinleck was already benefiting from an enhanced level of support that Wavell had craved. Rommel, meanwhile, could only mutter darkly about the German High Command assuming that the new kit they were sending always arrived, when the truth was that almost half was never reaching the units for whom it was destined.

With Tobruk still his intended prize, Rommel was using all his knowledge of military tactics and applying them to his parlous supply situation, then adding liberal amounts of his own determination to achieve personal goals. He used his time to re-structure his forces and to plan as he had never planned before. In Africa he was setting the day-to-day agenda rather than, as in the fall of France, following the orders of others. For once, he was stopping and thinking, and it paid dividends in building a force that was organised and decently equipped; the lack of substantial action had meant no major losses of military equipment.

As winter approached, Field Marshal Albert Kesselring came to join Rommel in the region. He was a Bavarian gunnery officer who had transferred to the fledgling Luftwaffe and would eventually succeed Rommel and organise the withdrawal from the African theatre. At Hitler's direction, the newcomer was to repair the sad state of the convoy traffic across the Mediterranean. Though he quickly formed the same view as Rommel about the Italian commitment to the cause, he also soon appreciated that no army could fight for long on the level of supplies that was reaching the German-held ports in Africa. He also realised that Rommel's next moves were vital to future fortunes in the area and that consistent re-supply was essential. His impact was considerable and quick, with the Luftwaffe becoming more involved in both offensive and protective duties.

By now, Rommel was in charge of Panzer Group Afrika, a new designation for the combination of Crüwell's Afrika Corps comprising 15th and 20th Panzer Divisions, 90th Light Division and the Sarona Division, and Navarrini's XXI Italian Corps made up of the Trento, Bologna, Brescia and Pavia Divisions. For the first time since his arrival, Axis forces in North Africa had co-ordination and structure.

Rommel deployed his forces so that he could concentrate on Tobruk without fear of attacks to his rear. He then spent all daylight hours racing around the front to keep his men in full concentration, using the carrot of compliments and humour and the stick of fierce criticism when he saw error or slackness. He also ensured the state of readiness was retained by dint of regular and tough training routines.

For one who had left his own training years far behind and, apart from keeping abreast of developments in tank and weaponry performance, relied much on intuition, the Panzer general's attention was now unusually focused on ensuring that the tank and artillery crews were completely ready for the upcoming battles. Those who criticise him for what they consider his superficial approach to the theory of warfare would do well to observe his attention to detail at this point. He appeared to be compensating for what he deemed to be a shortage of men and machines by ensuring what he did have was ready and able to perform at its very best.

Rommel was planning for a whole-hearted attempt to capture Tobruk in the third week of November and issued orders to that effect on 26 October. It can now be seen that Rommel, never one to overly concern himself with the plans the enemy might have, had been completely ignoring Allied intentions to the degree that he was barely aware of the Intelligence reports of British movements or was, at least, feigning ignorance of them to maintain enthusiasm among his men, especially the Italians whom he still viewed likely to move into full retreat at the first whisper of a threat! He was sure, and rightly so, that Tobruk would be no easy capture. As he had used the recent quiet period to plan, so too, he knew, had the Allies who, in comparison, had been landing new tanks, guns and trucks at will.

Newly arrived on the scene was General Alan Cunningham, recruited by Auchinleck to encourage broader and faster battlefield deployment. Both he and General Godwin-Austen, now in charge of XIII Corps, had been in East Africa, and General Norrie had come from England to replace Lieutenant-General Vyvyan Pope, a tank specialist killed in a recent air crash. Thus, the Allied cause was in the hands of relative novices to desert conditions while Rommel could count on the experience of such as Generals Bayerlein and Crüwell.

At least Cunningham was initially cautious and so avoided inviting German counter-attacks that could have been damaging.

Operation 'Crusader'

This was to be the first battle of the fledgling Eighth Army and it would begin the campaign with Churchillian exhortations to glory echoing in the ears of the large force assembled by the British leader, at the expense of other theatres. It would be this new Army that would put the horrors of the failure of Operation 'Battleaxe' behind it.

The Eighth Army, under Cunningham, would begin 'Crusader' with some 118,000 men, marginally more than the combined German and Italian forces of 100,000; there was Allied superiority in tank numbers too, with 455 to Rommel's 412, of which many were inferior Italian types. The German vehicles, however, were vastly superior, the British machines suffering from ineffective firepower, poor reliability and weak construction when facing the awesome German 50mm and 75mm guns.

When 'Crusader' began on 18 November, the Allies, to avoid Rommel powering directly for Alexandria, chose not to concentrate their attacks to the south but rather to push towards Tobruk, with feinting diversions elsewhere. Some early advantage was achieved, for if Rommel believed that the relief of Tobruk was the primary aim, the greater plan to push Rommel far back and out of Cyrenaica and Tripolitania might be kept undisclosed for longer. Tactics were crucial if a punishing face-to-face fire-fight with the powerful German tanks was to be avoided.

Rommel's force for 'Crusader' was numerically dominated by Italian personnel and consisted of two motorised and five infantry divisions as well as its three armoured formations, and at the start-point he was still suffering hugely through the efforts of the British air and sea attacks on his re-supply convoys across the Mediterranean; Kesselring's worthy efforts had yet to bear much fruit. His planning had been thorough but he was still hamstrung by the inadequacies of his mongrel force and his ability to fight a long action. Operation 'Crusader' was to see him at his intuitive best and his spiritual worst.

The battle immediately became fierce; it represented one of the greatest tank actions of these early war years. It also produced one of Erwin Rommel's most discussed battlefield manoeuvres. Allied armour quickly gained control of the airfield at Sidi Rezegh, but became embroiled in costly battles at Gabr Saleh and Bir el Gubi. In counter, Rommel sought out these British armoured units and began to inflict great damage until Cunningham finally sent reinforcements on 22 November.

Whilst the British were losing tanks too easily, they did have replacements in reserve whereas Rommel, when Crüwell lost many in a token victory at Sidi Rezegh on the 23rd, found his stock being reduced without hope of replenishment. Now, showing his readiness to act 'on the hoof,' the Swabian changed his plans completely by suddenly turning his armour to the east and heading for the Egyptian border, the 'dash to the wire'. His intention to cause panic and confusion in the Allied ranks very nearly worked, and might have done but for Auchinleck's promptness in flying in from Cairo to replace the lack-lustre Cunningham with Neil Ritchie and demanding that the offensive be followed through.

But what was the purpose behind Rommel's sudden change of plan? In truth his options were limited if he was to retain his short-term goal of taking Tobruk. He had to turn to his strength – his panzer divisions – and chose to do so in a manner that would threaten the Allied rear, cause chaos to the opposition's communications and bring about an Allied withdrawal. Despite the fact that his men subsequently passed within a mile of so of two massive Allied fuel dumps and yet did not destroy them, the strategy came very close to working; in fact it did work, but not completely. It was a daring plan concocted as the battle raged around him and shows us just how adaptable a battlefield commander Rommel was.

Despite the curious affair of the fuel stores where it seems a simple matter of weak Intelligence was to blame for the failure to capture or destroy them,

Rommel's moves certainly brought Cunningham close to calling off the contest and only Auchinleck's intervention prevented it.

Rommel, seeing that his bluff had been called and concerned at his lack of fuel and support, turned again and headed for Tobruk. Weakened by reversals around Sidi Rezegh, the Allies concentrated on cutting the Axis escape routes to the west and immediately secured a decision from Rommel to withdraw his siege of Tobruk in order to at least gather his force again at Gazala, which he had done by 11 December. He was still being hassled by the enemy and was obliged to break out on 16 December and strike across the desert towards the Tripolitanian boundary, and he did so with sufficient pace to keep ahead of the Allied pursuers and link up with some reinforcements from Benghazi.

Before crossing the border at the year's end, Rommel secured another victory against the forward units of his pursuers to ensure that he escaped this period of conflict with some credibility. He had inflicted significant losses on the enemy and been shown to have a more considered plan than that with which his opposition had set out. He had, however, lost two-thirds of his men killed, wounded or captured compared to barely 15 per cent losses among the Allies. His excellent tanks had not held sway, the Italian machines had been inadequate, but he had survived, bloodied but unbowed, to fight for Tobruk and give Kesselring time to engineer a change of fortune on the supply front.

The final judgement on Operation 'Crusader' can be best described as an honourable draw that could have been more successful for either side. It was partly successful for the British in that they took numbers of prisoners and removed many Axis men and machines from the battle-zone, but the Afrika Korps had survived to fight

Rommel talks with the German CinC South, Albert Kesselring. The latter was expected to improve the supply situation, but enjoyed only limited success.

another day. Rommel's forces had not gained the initiative as he had wanted and he was not able to keep to his schedule for capturing Tobruk, but he had, in Auchinleck's own words, given his opponents a 'rude shock' by his change of tactics in mid-battle. If the Allied commanders had been uncertain beforehand, they knew now that they faced a most resourceful and imaginative foe.

As they licked their 'Crusader' wounds, both desert combatants looked to the supply situation. The British had found their armour hopelessly inadequate compared to the German machines and would press for better equipment to arrive soon. Rommel had used every last piece of land armour and had run perilously close to bringing about his defeat by this very fact; he now looked to Kesselring to get supplies through and, if he did, the Swabian remained confident of success.

Gazala and Tobruk

When units of the Eighth Army made contact with the Tobruk garrison during Operation 'Crusader', a deep sigh of relief was to be heard among the Allied forces in the desert and in London too. But the resilient Rommel still knew that he needed the fortified port to further his North African ambitions and, despite his huge losses of men and machines, and the losses in January of Bardia, Sollum, Halfaya and other frontier positions, he chose to attack, just three weeks into the new year. He had lost 80 per cent of his aircraft, more than 90 per cent of his tanks and well over half his men; no reinforcements could be expected for weeks, perhaps months, so why attack, what could he achieve?

Erwin Rommel was surely as exhausted and dispirited as his men and he, like his opponents, craved a peaceful interlude after two months' continual fighting. Both sides needed to re-group and plan. This is why the German attacked, for he always sought the advantage and unconventional decisions had often given him that. With barely 120 battleworthy tanks, including 54 newly arrived armoured vehicles and little air cover, he set out with the remnant of his Afrika Korps and, using the benefit of surprise, brushed aside Allied units encountered in the first thrusts. Buoyed by early success Rommel ploughed into the Allied newcomers of 1st Armoured Division who were promptly decimated by an enemy they had been told was 'licking his wounds'. In just two weeks German forces swept past Msus, encircled and took Benghazi, by-passed Derna and were threatening Gazala and Tobruk yet again. The Allies were forced back behind their minefields running south from Gazala to Bir Hacheim. This German offensive had covered more than 300 miles but cost Rommel barely thirty tanks; it was a short and simple testimony to the man's courage and élan.

It was at this time that the war was taking a different path in various theatres. On the Allied side the problems in the Far East were beginning to cause distractions in London and in North Africa where the 18th Division, once intended to swell resources there, was diverted to Singapore, only to be captured and imprisoned without seeing action. Churchill was desperate to keep Mediterranean waters clear for his convoys to the desert, but these shipments were also being reduced because the *matériel* was needed elsewhere. The German situation, by comparison, showed signs of improving. With Kesselring in place and German High Command somewhat more committed to Rommel's cause, Malta came under increasing air attack, and Allied shipping no longer sailed an unfettered route from Gibraltar. Now it was Axis aircraft and submarines that held sway and German supplies that got through.

Allied command in Africa was in a quandary. It could ill afford to attack incoming German replenishments for risk of losing its own equipment needed for larger actions, but it faced the prospect of losing Malta if nothing was done. If it lost that vital staging post then it was effectively sacrificing the whole of the Mediterranean and, with that, Egypt and the Middle East. The compromise agreed was that more equipment and men would be found for a new offensive in mid-May, subsequently delayed by one month, though the success of this would still depend on the ability to keep Malta available.

Since Rommel's New Year race back towards Gazala, the Eighth Army had spent time strengthening its defensive line there. A fifty-mile run of fortifications and minefields was created which it was thought would deter even the 'Desert Fox'. It was considered that Rommel, despite the fresh supplies he was receiving, would not be ready to mount an offensive before the Allies themselves could attack, but this confidence was ill-placed.

Erwin Rommel had 'sat on his hands' long enough and launched his next offensive on 26 May, some three weeks before the Allies could have been ready. He employed a tactic very typical of him. A small force – Italians troops in this case – was launched against his opponents' main line while he raced to the south of the fortified line with his 15th and 21st Panzer Divisions, the 90th Light Division and the Ariete and Trieste Divisions of the Italian XX Corps. From a point at the end of the Allied defences at Bir Hacheim, these latter units were intended to turn north and head for Tobruk, moving *behind* the main body of Allied forces.

The Allied defensive 'boxes' were intended to protect the minefields and prevent the cutting of swathes through them. By stopping the enemy as he tried to break through, the Allied artillery could effect much damage, causing retreat or providing the opportunity for counter-attack. This was logical; common military sense dictated that the German route to Tobruk, for all knew this was the prize that Rommel still sought, was through this barrier. But Rommel was capable of discarding the probable in favour of the possible more readily than any other commander in the war. As we shall discover in a later chapter, his moves at Gazala were constantly quicker, more effective and less formal than those employed by his opponents, and for this reason he 'won' the great prize of Tobruk.

The port fell on 21 June and the supplies it was protecting allowed Rommel to press on to the Egyptian border 48 hours later, albeit with fewer than sixty tanks. The Allies had moved back 120 miles to Mersa Matruh and would eventually withdraw the same distance again, to El Alamein where Auchinleck would prepare the next defensive line.

For his achievements at Gazala and Tobruk, Erwin Rommel was promoted to Field Marshal. He was forty-nine years of age, Germany's youngest officer of this rank, and he celebrated his promotion with a feast of tinned pineapple and a small glass of whisky from a bottle taken from the Tobruk NAAFI.[10]

The First Battle of El Alamein

The priority of the Allies now was to stave off any enemy attacking moves towards Alexandria and Cairo. At El Alamein the gap between the sea and the impenetrable Qattara Depression and its quicksands was just forty miles and Field Marshal Rommel would have to get through it if he was to reach these next objectives.

Having been outwitted and mauled by Rommel at Gazala and Tobruk, the hapless General Ritchie, who was to perform creditably later in the war but had been ill-placed in the desert of which he had no experience, was removed by Auchinleck. The latter took direct control of the retreat to Alamein and the creation of a new defensive line there, but he was given little time by his German opponent for Rommel was at the line by the end of June and launched his first attack the following day.

It was now that the new Field Marshal began to believe his own press. Certainly he was receiving congratulatory comments from German High Command, his effective use of the Italian forces was even bringing praise from Rome, and he had seen time and again how slow the Allied forces were to prepare their next moves. Surely all he needed to do now was use his improved supply situation and the confident mood of his own men to knock on the Alamein defences and watch them fall.

Claude Auchinleck had other plans. Although much of his armour was only reaching his lines just ahead of the Germans, he was able to launch a counterattack against Rommel's first thrusts on 1 July that captured a new fort south of El Alamein at Deir el Shein. He continued to mount short, sharp attacks that shook the Axis forces by their strength and purpose. An initial German sortie on the strategically significant Ruweisat Ridge was twice repulsed and Allied units took control of part of that feature and held off further attempts to regain the ground.

In the latter half of the month the Australian and New Zealand Divisions attempted to break through and divide the German ranks and, though they were unsuccessful, and prompted Auchinleck to abandon further offensives for the time being, their effect caused Rommel likewise to step back rather than further risk his limited tank and fuel resources. It had been an exhausting few weeks for all combatants and it was unsurprising that each side felt the need to pause and take stock.

The North Africa theatre was tough enough for any commander and Rommel's arrival there had certainly caused some to be found wanting in their ability to counter his bravado and speed of thought and movement. At this point Auchinleck was expecting to begin planning what offensive moves he could make, perhaps by September, when the 44th Infantry Division, newly arrived in the region, would be ready to fight. But it was not to be, for General Alexander planned to bring General Bernard Montgomery in to replace 'the Auk', delay the next attacks to allow for two further Divisions and more, and newer, tanks and guns to arrive. Auchinleck returned to India not knowing what he might have achieved had he been allowed to work with the benefits Montgomery was about to enjoy or hearing the compliments of his enemies – of whom he had captured more than 7,000 in a little over three weeks – on the matter of the fighting performance of his men and the effectiveness of his tactics during July. He was gone, and Erwin Rommel was about to face his toughest battlefield opponent.

We now know what a parlous state Rommel was in when hostilities closed at the end of July. He had no heavy artillery ammunition, few tanks and was prepared to withdraw if the Allies had mounted one more large attack. He had no option other than to stop fighting, but it is ironic that his opponents felt the same and had no inkling that one further offensive drive could have brought significant success. This is, however, another sign of Rommel's lack of concern for the logistics of the battlefield; his was a soldier's mind, not a clerk's, and he could seldom be encouraged to think of campaign administration. He could have paused longer at Tobruk, rested his troops, enjoyed the fruits of securing this supply base, and then moved forward with greater strength and forward planning, but it was not his way. 'Why give the enemy time to regroup when I have the ascendancy?' was his thinking, and, to this point, it had served him well.

Having said that, Rommel was forever campaigning for more men and *matériel*. The German High Command, and its Italian equivalent, received constant requests – more usually curt demands – but could usually reply only with promises and words of encouragement. The Swabian held the view that his capabilities as a commander were nullified if he was under-equipped, but that, better supplied, he could be master of any battlefield situation.

Now, as the year dragged on, his securing of Tobruk was not seen to garner the result he had been promised. The massed Axis action against the Malta convoys and the island itself had dented but not ended this vital Allied supply route. The suspension of sailings in July was lifted when Operation 'Pedestal', with its 20 warships, fourteen merchant vessels, 32 destroyers, other craft and the aircraft carrier *Furious* with fighter aircraft on board, left Scotland and headed for the Mediterranean. Almost constant air attacks from Sardinia and Sicily and by submarines caused great damage to the fleet, but sufficient remnants got through to Malta in mid-August amid great rejoicing from the three British armed services, the Maltese people and Alexander and Montgomery as they planned their moves against the 'Desert Fox'.

The situation facing Montgomery was that he believed an attack would come from the German earlier rather than later, in other words, before he himself was ready to move. This was based on the belief that the Axis situation was better than it actually was, though he could not see how Rommel could attempt a drive all the way to Cairo or the Nile Delta. In fact, although the German still had better armour (but numerically weaker than his opponent), his forces were numerically strong only because six of his divisions were Italian, and the Royal Air Force still had control of the air. Furthermore, his innate battlefield skill was nullified by the geography of the Alamein area which made an attack around his enemy to its rear, his long preferred practice, only possible by sea or via any weakness he could force on the flanks of the Allied defensive line.

It was now that the value of thorough planning, rather than setting tactics on a whim, came into play. Alexander and Montgomery had studied their German adversary, the terrain, the positions both sides held, and other strengths and weaknesses. They knew that any attempted breakthrough would have to come through the southern sector, and that Rommel must be opposed by very different strategies than those used against him in the past if he was to be defeated. Montgomery saw to it that the German acquired an apparently genuine map of the area south of Alam Halfa that indicated the ground there was good for armoured traffic when, in fact, it was soft and wholly unsuitable. He also ensured that any attempt by Rommel to get through this sector of the line would be quickly met by a severe secondary test; he fortified the Alam Halfa Ridge to such a degree – using the whole of 44th Division – that it could play both a defensive and an attacking role as required. He knew that Rommel could not afford to by-pass it, was ensuring he would have to fight long and hard for it, and gave himself the option of counter-attacking from this stronghold if the opportunity arose. He also positioned 7th Armoured Division some fifteen miles behind the front-line in the south.

Alam Halfa

On 30 August Rommel made his expected move. Under cover of darkness and with modest diversionary attacks farther north, he drove his main forces into the Allied line between Bab el Qattara and the El Taqa plateau, but his initial success brought him face-to-face with 7th Armoured and forced him where he did not immediately want to go, straight at Alam Halfa Ridge and 22 Armoured Brigade stationed at its south-western edge. The German had entered the fray with 440 tanks of which more than half were the less valuable Italian machines; they faced more than 700 Allied tanks which including American Grants.

If he was shocked by having his direction of advance dictated by his enemy, Rommel did not immediately show it. Indeed, he showed his ability to change tactics on the move when he attempted to outflank 22 Armoured only to find the anti-tank defences vastly improved on what he had encountered before. His forces were again suffering from a shortage of fuel and other supplies and were being constantly harassed by Allied aircraft which flew more than 3,000 missions; it appeared his latest adventure was to fail within days.

The German rightly chose to withdraw to where he had started. Thus, from the great success of Gazala and Tobruk, he had quickly tasted a major reversal and it was more than just that for he had encountered a new and apparently more sophisticated and considered strategy, though it was not all of Montgomery's doing. He had been completely unaware of the strengthening of Alam Halfa and the positioning of 7th Armoured Division, and was not used to

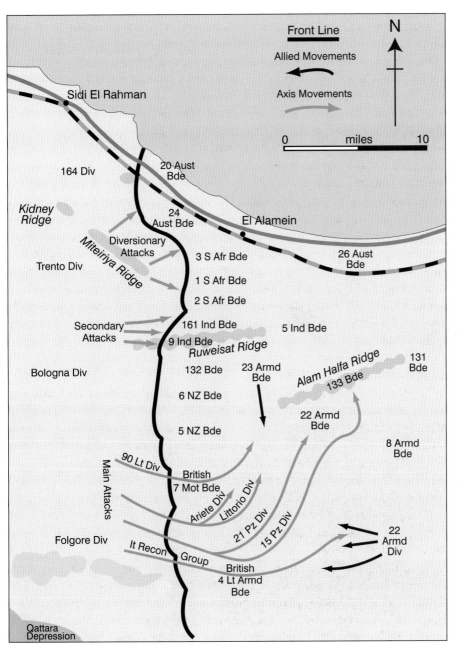

BATTLE OF ALAM HALFA, 31 AUGUST TO 1 SEPTEMBER 1942

being guided round the battlefield as and when the opposition required. The Allied air attacks broke the momentum of the advance and the impact of Kesselring on the theatre appeared to have been all too short-lived.

Although Rommel now resolved to reinforce the defensive positions opposite the Allied lines, he was not happy. Mentally and physically at a new low, the euphoria of capturing Tobruk was fast becoming a dim memory in a darkening sky. He could not withdraw further for fear of complete annihilation; once on the move, he would have inadequate vehicles and fuel to keep ahead of the enemy. His latest initiative had been destroyed inside a week; he was back where he had started from, having suffered significant losses and with no hope of mounting further attacks without a major re-supply of tanks and fuel.

He flew back to Germany for medical treatment but still took the opportunity of a meeting with Hitler to assure him that only the re-supply of men, fuel and armour was preventing him from taking Alexandria, Cairo, the whole of Egypt and moving forward the southern flank of the grand German plan for the Middle East, the Balkans and the Caucasus. The assurances the Führer gave him, including the exciting promise of new shallow-draught barges to overcome the fuel supply problem, were vague and undeliverable, though the examples he was shown of the new Tiger tank and a multiple mortar were real enough. The Swabian had suffered long enough from these false dawns and he left the meeting in the belief that everything that had been said to him had been to quieten his rebellious attitude. What he did not appreciate was that the decision had been taken to remove him from North Africa.

The plan of High Command was that Rommel would be given command of an Army Group in the southern Ukraine, a move explained to him before he entered hospital as one aimed at giving him a change of climate. It was not to be, however, because his replacement, General Stumme, was immediately found wanting and the 'Fox' was invited to return to his territory.

Erwin Rommel was a man of his nation and a national hero; it was never likely that he would refuse the invitation even though his medical treatment remained incomplete. It would be a weak Field Marshal who walked unsteadily to his aircraft early one morning, straight from hospital, to begin the arduous trip back to North Africa which, despite stops in Italy and Crete, he still reached by the evening. Before he arrived the Allies were already making their moves.

One of the first tasks of Bernard Montgomery was to give a victory to the battered Allied troops in the desert, and he had achieved that at Alamein at the end of June and again at Alam Halfa. His second priority was to get the next action properly planned and the officers and men fully committed to the scheme. Such had been the turnover of senior officers since the outset of the Allied campaign that evidence of permanence and good order was vital. Part of this studied approach was to gather together the best possible logistic support and all the ammunition and armour that could be mustered, and then to use them to the maximum effect. If there was to be a second battle at El Alamein the diminutive British General was determined it would end in his favour.

The Second Battle of El Alamein

North Africa remained the only war theatre in which Germany was not dominant so the significance of an Axis victory when the opponents next faced one another there was vital to Rommel. He strove to conceive a way in which he could give his nation the victory it craved and remained confident in his own ability to obtain the best performance from his men and thus give the Axis forces the best possible chance of success. But would that be enough against an army that appeared now to be in the hands of a more judicious battlefield commander who was blessed with a far superior supply situation than himself.

Before his trip to Germany, Rommel had laid out the defensive positions the Axis forces were to take up. These involved 15th Panzer Division monitoring the north and 21st Panzer Division in the south, and still included substantial numbers of Italian troops. The German contingent was more used to being driven forward by their beloved Field Marshal and had come to loathe inaction as much as he; the Italians were also unhappy with their situation though this was based more on their anticipation of the toughness of the next battle than the urge to be involved in it. The Field Marshal was returning to a damaged force.

As he had proved more than once in his military career to date, Erwin Rommel was capable of winning battles, from small skirmishes to major actions, when numbers of men and weapons were against him. His personal energy and intuitive battlefield decision-making seemed to correct the imbalance on several occasions and the pace of his movement caught many unawares. This was a time, however, where formal planning and military theory would be made to count; added to a formula that included such dominance in numbers of men and equipment it might have been deemed 'No contest'.

The equation for this decisive battle was forbidding. Rommel had half the number of men and a third the number of tanks that Montgomery had at his disposal, and the Allied Desert Air Force was dominant over his struggling air support. He still lacked fuel and, at this point, was still sharing the scene with General Stumme who had been sent to replace him. All he could claim was that his defensive positions were well established all along the line from the sea to the Qattara Depression; but was this also a negative factor, had he spread his resources too thinly?

Both sides had now suffered the physical hardships of desert fighting for longer than was desirable, though the Allied armies numbered more recent arrivals than their enemy's. Conditions for normal daily life were bad enough – ferocious heat and flies by the thousand were just two of the trials faced by men who were used to neither – and the natural desire for comfort, a warm bath or shower, and regular meals had long since been replaced by one which modestly craved the pleasures of one's home country. The Allies had undoubtedly been buoyed by Montgomery's arrival for while he bore the pale skin of a desert new-comer, they quickly saw evidence of more determination and planning, and heard believable words of encouragement in his squeaky, high-pitched voice. The German troops had been shaken by the reversals at El Alamein and Alam Halfa, and the senior staff, at least, knew their commander had been away on sick leave.

Montgomery's preparation for the next battle, one that he was determined would put an end once and for all to the German threat to the Suez Canal, was extreme by any standards. He had arrived in North Africa to find what he described as gross mismanagement and dreadful staff work, but now he had to design a battle scenario that would bring about the decisive victory – it was a theme he returned to constantly as he implemented his plans with senior officers.

For weeks the Allies sought to mislead German Intelligence by suggesting they were undertaking a slow build-up to the south of their lines. Hundreds of dummy vehicles were placed at strategic points to suggest the creating of field HQs and supply points and a mock pipeline was built in the same direction. These extraordinary steps were taken in parallel with more subdued moves in the north where such vehicles as were moved forward were immediately cam-ouflaged, tanks being disguised with painted canvas to resemble trucks.

Montgomery also benefited from a major new asset as the battle approached. The British decoding offices at Bletchley Park in Buckinghamshire had cracked the German Enigma code machines to the degree that German messages sent around this theatre could now be quickly translated by the Ultra system and placed in front of the Allied commanders. As a result almost every Axis convoy bound for North Africa was attacked, resulting in nearly 70 per cent of the intended replenishments failing to get through. On the other hand, a major Allied convoy arrived in September and the Desert Air Force continued to dom-inate the skies, including those above the Mediterranean.

Rommel, as ever, was endeavouring to think positively when he arrived back in North Africa on 24 October, but he had already received the bad news of an Allied attack being mounted. At 0940 the day before, some 600 British guns had begun a withering bombardment ahead of the first troop move-ments; it was like a Blitzkrieg attack and that was not the only similarity to a Rommel strategy. Montgomery had successfully feinted his move to the south but had marshalled his main force far to the north, and he had indeed added to the confusion by placing numerous dummy vehicles in potential gathering points of attack and slowly created many mock dumps in the south in order to suggest a more cautious build-up than was actually the case. False radio messages were broadcast and the dummy pipelines, along with limited recon-naissance flights being possible by the Luftwaffe – a greater number might have disclosed the trickery below – meant that the Germans, including the returning Rommel, must have felt justified in setting the broad defensive line they had. The messages that did get passed to Rommel and his officers by German Intelligence were worse than useless.

It would be three days after the first attack that Rommel would truly take back control of the situation – Stumme was to die from a heart-attack while being driven around the battlefield during an Allied attack – and he would be quick to concede the battle was surely lost. Even so, he would strive to do what he could

BATTLE OF EL ALAMEIN, 23 OCTOBER TO 4 NOVEMBER 1942

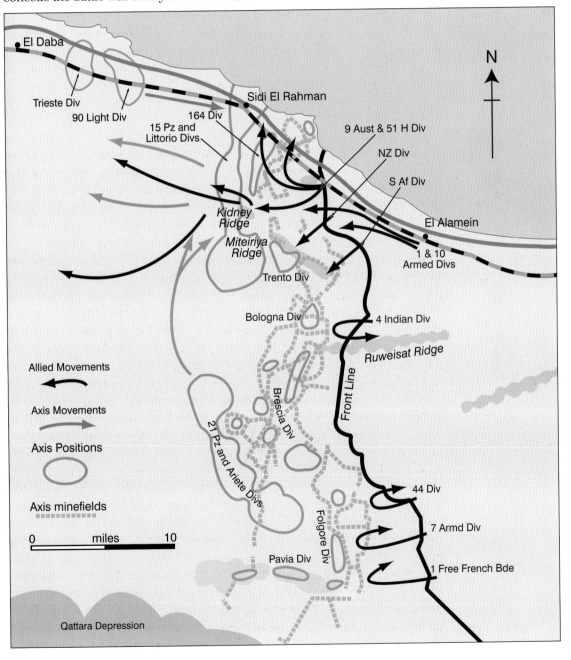

- El Daba
- Trieste Div
- 90 Light Div
- Sidi El Rahman
- 164 Div
- 15 Pz and Littorio Divs
- 9 Aust & 51 H Div
- NZ Div
- S Af Div
- Kidney Ridge
- Miteiriya Ridge
- El Alamein
- 1 & 10 Armed Divs
- Trento Div
- Bologna Div
- 4 Indian Div
- Ruweisat Ridge
- Front Line
- Brescia Div
- 21 Pz and Ariete Divs
- 44 Div
- Folgore Div
- 7 Armd Div
- Pavia Div
- 1 Free French Bde
- Qattara Depression

N

Allied Movements

Axis Movements

Axis Positions

Axis minefields

0   miles   10

by quickly supplementing the devastated 15th Panzer in the north with 21st Panzer from the south and 90th Light Division from the west. Just 48 hours after leaving his hospital bed in Germany he was leading a vigorous armoured counter-attack against the salient caused by the rapid Allied push along the coast.

It is tempting to consider how different this Alamein battle might have been had Rommel been present from the outset. The defensive disposition of the Axis forces was the one he had decreed and its inadequacy in dealing with the first Allied thrusts was therefore his fault. But it was a close run thing, with the tortuous progress through the extensive minefields proving an awesome trial for the British and Commonwealth troops. One has the feeling, however, that a fit and present 'Desert Fox' would have reacted more promptly and vigorously to Montgomery's first moves; he would not have allowed his opponents such gains as they achieved in the first 48 hours.

These gains, brought about more by fierce resolution and a new belief that the enemy was close to defeat rather than simply because of the unexpected direction of the chosen route, were achieved literally inch by inch, because Rommel's minefields had been designed by one who knew what depth of defence would have been necessary to deter himself. The formidable German guns, combined with the night-time attack and the sluggish advance of the tank force behind them, meant that the Allied infantry were not through the mines by the end of the first night as planned and had to dig themselves into whatever shallow cover they could while they waited to move again under cover of darkness.

The men in the minefields would not have heard Montgomery's final talk to his officers, held in a cinema, but they would have been told that his message was that there would be only one result to this battle, that the enemy would be 'hit for six out of Africa'. It must have seemed less than certain as they kept their heads down in the sparse, flat landscape, knowing that one false movement could bring an artillery shell. A force of 150,000 troops had begun the tedious crawl in the cool of the night, now those who had survived faced a fearful day in the desert sun; each man knew that if he survived this phase of the operation, he would still have to fight the enemy. The failure of the force to get through on this first night suggests that Montgomery's tactics had not worked, but he expressed a determination that it should continue and succeed. He was calm enough to regroup and press for a fresh effort when many would have tried to complete the work in daylight or cancel it altogether.

The advance was completed during the following nights and these troops engaged the enemy in some fierce close-quarter fighting. Many of the tanks that followed them through the gaps in the minefield were picked off by Rommel's guns, still devastatingly accurate as they had to be when so short of supplies. An entire fuel convoy was lost as it crept along its dangerous route. This five-mile advance through one of the most dense minefields ever laid – it included anti-personnel devices as well as anti-tank mines – is rightly the stuff of legend and it showed a level of resolve that shook the Germans and their Field Marshal.

The impetus was with the Allies now. Rommel had initially been too occupied with moving 21st Panzer and Ariete Divisions north and reforming defensive positions to work on replacing the massive armour losses he had already suffered, but he did raise the spirits and determination of his men. In the short term all he could do was make the enemy fight for every inch of territory and he did counter attack on the 26th and 27th, Alexander recording that it was only three days into the battle that the enemy finally concentrated all his resources against the real attack.

At this point the Eighth Army had lost 10,000 men without securing victory and there was a fear that the attack was losing its momentum as the forward drive got bogged down in minor delaying skirmishes. It was now that Montgomery sent the Australian 9th Division along the coast road, causing Rommel to commit the 90th Light Division to counter it, but this was only a preliminary to Operation 'Supercharge' that was launched against the Italian Trento Division on 2 November.

General von Thoma, commander of the Afrika Korps at the time of the decisive Alamein battle, is seen after capture.

At last the Allies' huge press forward achieved the breakthrough. More than 15,000 shells were fired ahead of infantry advances which, with tank support, finally got to Rommel's anti-tank guns that had so pummelled the hapless Commonwealth units. Using his new American tanks to maximum effect, Montgomery made life a misery for the fuel-starved Axis tank commanders. Even so, 9th Armoured Division had lost three-quarters of a brigade before the extra tank power outnumbered Rommel in a day-long battle. Facing continued crippling attacks from the skies and with only a few dozen tanks operational, Rommel sent a message to Hitler saying that all was lost and that he had no alternative but to withdraw. Despite his leader's response calling for a 'last stand', the 'Desert Fox' knew that he must make for Tripoli at best pace before the anticipated arrival of the new Allied armies landing in north-west Africa in Operation 'Torch' made even that thankless move impossible.

Rommel chose to circulate copies of the Führer's call to 'hold El Alamein to the last man' among his troops. Perhaps he felt a decision to withdraw, thus choosing to give up the vision of victory in North Africa, was too great for him to take, and all in the German Army knew the ramifications of disregarding a directive from the Führer. Some commanders were already moving their troops back only to find Allied units were blocking their path; General von Thoma, commanding the Afrika Korps, was one who fell into this trap and was captured.

To his commanders who sought clear direction from their Field Marshal, the Swabian was dour and non-committal, telling them he could not openly counter-

General Alexander's message to Churchill as shown in the Army Film Unit's *Desert Victory*.

mand Hitler's order but agreeing that everyone must ignore it if lives were to be saved. Erwin Rommel was beaten, broken and in worse health than he realised, but even in this dark mood he still summoned up enough spirit to organise the retreat the best he could. On 4 November the withdrawal began, and was immediately faced with the inevitability of further major losses as there was insufficient transport, fuel or armour protection to secure the route for the numbers involved. Large swathes of Italian personnel were quickly captured.

Matters could have been worse but for the heavy rain that prevented Allied forces getting to Mersa Matruh to encircle the remaining German composite division. Montgomery was making no substantial effort to block the German withdrawal and was typically cautious in arranging a whole-hearted pursuit, perhaps because he and his men too were somewhat drained by the huge effort of recent days. Eventually the pursuit did get underway and was sufficiently robust to prevent Rommel pausing to make a fresh stand.

For Rommel, the big battle at El Alamein had proved as decisive as it appeared to have been for the Allies. Because of his wretched supply situation he had been losing more armour and men with every initiative he launched, he had suddenly faced new and impressive American tanks without being forewarned by his Intelligence people, and he had come up against an opposing commander who, given his new numbers of men and machines, had shown tactical acumen and fighting spirit that the German had not previously encountered in the whole of his military career. The Swabian who had enjoyed such success and acclaim throughout his life, had now suffered his most ignominious defeat.

He led his men on a sorry route that would see them hurry west for sanctuary and, he hoped, the opportunity to fight again.

Rommel's Last Days in Africa

Any hopes that Erwin Rommel had that he would fight again in Africa – and win – were ended when the 'Torch' landings in north-west Africa on 8 November were reported as being successful; nothing could now prevent whatever force he could muster being caught in the middle of two advancing armies. As he led his diminished force westwards, the men and their charismatic leader in the lowest of spirits, he found no position where he could set up an effective defensive line with his inadequate resources. Tripoli was sacrificed with only minimal fighting and, though the long promised reinforcements of men and machines now began to arrive, not even the appearance of the new Tiger tank and 10th Panzer Division could change the position.

The 'Desert Fox' was recalled to Germany where he found himself accused by his Führer of being an habitual loser who disobeyed orders, and being told in the one-sided interview that only his apparent loyalty stopped him from being treated as those guilty of such sins in the manner others had been – of being stood against a wall and shot. He was told to return to Africa and use his increased resources rather better, and to recover Tripoli.

We know that Rommel asked Hitler whether he was prepared to lose the Afrika Korps, as would happen if he attempted to re-take Tripoli, and got the response that the Afrika Korps came second to the ambitions of the nation. But we also know that, before Rommel left the room, his leader apologised for his outburst and suggested that they meet again next day. The second meeting included Göring who, during the session, was told by Hitler to provide Rommel with everything he needed for North Africa. But during the ensuing journey to Rome which was shared with his wife and Göring, the Swabian became convinced that nothing was going to be forthcoming and that the Reich was being led by a madman and an extravagant pursuer of personal luxury.

It was a sad and disillusioned Rommel who returned to North Africa, albeit one with increased personal status. He had been told that the German High Command could be persuaded that Tripoli might be lost, but that a new area of strength could be built up around the hinterland of Tunis and Bizerta. It was a foolish notion and one that Rommel had little sympathy with; it was another example of Hitler keeping too many fronts open at a time when consolidation was called for. There is little doubt that Rommel could have served Germany better at this time had he been given a significant position on the Eastern Front, but, as it was, he would have to oversee the gradual envelopment of his beloved Afrika Korps.

He still had one show of determination left in him however when, retiring to the Mareth Line just inside Tunisia, he at last found a location he could defend, one that would take a big effort on the part of the Allies to break through and would be a huge effort to outflank. Montgomery's progress in pursuit had been slow, to say the least, though this was partly due to the need to re-supply. Even Tripoli, re-entered at the end of January, was not functioning as a supply source until mid-March. Rommel had gained sufficient time and space to conjure up one last piece of battlefield enterprise.

As the Germans had been landing troops from Sicily by air and sea into Tunisia from November, Rommel was able to give the Allied forces spearheading the push forward from the 'Torch' landings a bloody nose at the Kasserine Pass. These were troops that had sailed and marched, but, as yet, barely fought and had certainly not defended a Rommel attack. In a miniature Blitzkrieg action he threw 21st Panzer Division backed by Stuka dive-bombers against the American armoured forces and made a nonsense of the haphazard defences that had been prepared at the Pass. Within hours he had punched a gaping hole through these fresh Allied forces and had created the tempting option of moving forward into the open.

An action that might have been planned to spread out Montgomery's force arriving from the east was now offering the enlivened Rommel the opportunity to cause a wholesale change of tactic among the 'Torch' arrivals. As it was, Alexander sent 6th Armoured Division forward with sufficient speed to strengthen the American line in time to discourage Rommel from advancing further, and by 22 February the German was re-tracing his steps to the Mareth Line and allowing Kasserine to fall back into Allied hands.

Erwin Rommel was nearly finished with the Desert, but he still had time for one more confrontation with Montgomery. On 6 March he launched 10th, 15th and 21st Panzer Divisions against the Allied lines with the aim of securing the large supply dumps at Medenine, but he was now up against stronger enemy forces and quickly lost more than 60 per cent of his 140 tanks without accounting for one of the opposition's. The Field Marshal used all his old means of encouraging his men, flitting around the battle points like a frenzied wasp looking for the right weak spot but it was all for nothing. The withering anti-tank gunfire ended the contest and the still ailing German had to give in to the inevitable.

It was on 12 March that Rommel was again recalled to Germany where he had another confrontation with the Führer. Although this was a full two months before High Command instructed Africa to be abandoned, there was no doubt in the mind of the departing Field Marshal that he would never return to this war theatre, and he must have regretted the call to leave. It was not in his nature to leave men behind when he left a battle-zone and there was no suspicion within the Afrika Korps that he had deserted them of his own volition. It was most certainly the case that the capture of Rommel, who had actually narrowly missed that fate by the skin of his teeth on several occasions, would have been

The wreckage of a German half-tracked troop carrier is inspected by Allied personnel.

a huge coup for the Allies and a massive reversal for the Germans. This surely explains his sudden departure.

In his absence the German forces began to face up to the pincer moves enveloping them from east and west. More than 70,000 men were lost as the combined German and Italian forces withdrew to within thirty miles of the Tunisian ports of Tunis and Bizerta, but, with the Allied First and Eighth Armies now joined, could not put off the inevitable for long. On 7 May units of 7th Armoured Division entered Tunis and five days later the German 90th Division surrendered near Enfidaville.

As the remnant of the Afrika Korps marched into captivity and the war in North Africa came to a close, it was left for both sides to ruminate on just how close the Germans had come to using it as an unlikely route to increasing their sphere of influence around the whole of the eastern Mediterranean and adjoining lands to the east and north. Was Alamein the turning-point? Could that battle have been won had Erwin Rommel been given adequate forces and *matériel*. Would the Allied strength, with the Americans included, although very late in the day, always have held sway? Would German victory at Alamein and quick successes into Egypt, Palestine and beyond have caused a suing for peace that would have changed the post-war map? Could Erwin Rommel have been the man who led that pervasive drive far beyond North Africa

What is certain is that Rommel as a battlefield leader achieved more success in the desert than Germany had the right to expect. Without competing adequately for the vital control route to this war theatre, the Third Reich never stood a chance of winning lasting control in North Africa. Hitler had remained committed to too many fronts and almost agreed with this argument when, in a more sanguine mood from which he had shown in their previous meetings, he met Rommel at his East Prussian headquarters in May. When asked by Rommel whether the full victory the Führer continued to speak of could still be won, Hitler replied, 'No'. He then went on to complain that no one would make peace with him.

Back to Europe

We have seen that Rommel was not fully fit during his last months in North Africa and this remained the case when he arrived back in Germany. His priority was a return to full health and then another command; this time, he expected, it would surely be the Eastern Front.

In the event he was posted to a 'desk' position as an adviser to the Führer, once he had completed his short convalescence. It appears that this was very much an *ad hoc* employment, not planned for nor carrying a specific remit, and it bored Rommel. He was no more enamoured of his next appointment, with Army Group B in northern Italy when that nation separated from its coalition with Germany, and it shows how disillusioned he was that he happily began his next assignment – to check on defences around the Danish coast.

At least this got the Swabian on the move again, and making a difference. With the specially selected Admiral Ruge at his side, Rommel dashed about and completed the Danish remit within ten days, then was promptly moved to the Channel coast of France. He was fighting no battles, except with the authorities and those who had been overseeing this work before his arrival, but he applied the same vigour. If these coastlines were to deter or delay an enemy invasion he would have to work hard and fast.

He was not, however, his own man for he was subordinate to Field Marshal von Rundstedt and they seldom were in accord, though neither was inclined to bring disagreements to a head. Soon the arrangements were clarified, with Rommel being made Commander-in-Chief of the German Armies in the sector from Holland to the Loire and thus empowered to undertake the strengthening of the coastal defences without hindrance, though his commitment to the value of static fortifications was not shared by Army Command or, indeed, the Navy.

Only someone with Rommel's verve and energy could have broken through the apathy of those above and from the men undertaking the actual work. The nature of command was not as cohesive and undisputed here as it had been in the Desert, but he did make a difference and it is the belief of some historians that, had he been given a few months longer for this work, Rommel would have made the job of the Allied invaders very much harder. He did what he could, but while he was preparing coastal defences, his famed British counterpart was part of the grand planning for the Allied effort of taking the war back to Germany. Where Montgomery's career still held the promise of further glories, Rommel's was stagnating.

Just as Rommel's African adventure suffered from lack of supplies, now his work around the French coasts was being similarly hampered, for example the concrete and steel needed for his endeavours was being taken for rocket sites. It meant, again, that he could not do his job as effectively as he would wish, and it was nothing to do with personal drive or ability. Nevertheless, he still laid twice as many mines as had been deployed in the previous three years, though he wanted to use more.

It is intriguing to look at the divergence of opinion throughout the German military on the value and purpose of static fortifications for it seems Rommel was an unlikely champion of the cause. His opinions stemmed from his own good Blitzkrieg experience in Europe and his less enjoyable time in Africa where he saw the awesome impact of effective air power. He was of the view that if the Allies gained a foothold on mainland Europe, sufficient to create their own air bases, then, unless Göring's increasingly dubious promises of new super aircraft came to fruition, the war would be lost. He was sure the answer was to prevent the enemy getting ashore.

This at first seems strange coming from a primary exponent of mobile battlefield warfare, but understandable when you appreciate it was more a definition of the man's broad understanding of the theory of warfare and a realisation of its multi-disciplinary nature. While the theory said that 3,000 miles of coastline could not be protected, especially without vastly greater numbers of troops and weapons, and that it was better to confront any invasion force where and when it landed, Rommel was firm in his belief that, in practice, with Allied air power likely to be dominant and all equipment having to be landed by the invasion force from slow, cumbersome landing-craft, the best option was to stop the attackers attempting a landing at all.

Perhaps von Rundstedt, a firm advocate of allowing the invasion force ashore where it could be pummelled by German armour and its supply source disrupted, knew that Rommel had been given too little time.

Whatever the arguments, the Allied commanders knew they had to plan for both eventualities. If Rommel was facing their invasion fleet they could expect him to undertake a three-pronged strategy of preventing them from landing if he could, driving them from the beaches if he could not, and securing a ring of defensive locations close to the landing area to stop the attempted breakout. It has to be remembered that Rommel was still a name to be respected in London for, if Eisenhower, Bradley and Patton had not yet faced him in battle, Montgomery had. The Englishman still remembered Dunkirk too, and the role the Swabian played there.

Whatever Rommel achieved before the invasion the Allies could expect to have to fight their way through a fusillade of shore-based artillery before they could gain the vital foothold. Then they expected to face an army directed and inspired by their Desert foe.

There followed as remarkable a confusion as has been seen in modern military and political command. Gerd von Rundstedt, the staunchly correct Prussian theorist, dependable and thorough, was convinced the Allies would land on the closest French landfall to the English coast – the Pas de Calais, just a couple of dozen miles from Kent and beneath the skies that had seen the air battles that prevented the German invasion in the other direction. Rommel and, incidentally, Adolf Hitler, both expected the Normandy beaches to be the site. Von Rundstedt had applied military theory, as had his staff colleagues, so Army command was almost in unison; Rommel and his leader had followed some other route to their decision – experience, gut reaction, and a natural preference for employing the unexpected.

The result was that already scarce resources were spread more thinly still. Rommel was given a trio of poor armoured divisions for the entire expanse from the Scheldt to the Atlantic coast, with Rundstedt retaining the rest in reserve to direct to the invasion point once it was known. Had Rommel's request to bring 12th SS Panzer Division to Normandy at the time he asked for it been agreed he might have stood a better chance, but, as it was, the Reich decision-making chain creaked into motion far too slowly and another error from above affected Rommel's battlefield performance.

When the invasion came, and succeeded, it was air superiority that gave it its impetus for, while the battles on to, across and away from the beaches were tortuous, the reinforcements that could have made it worse were prevented from reaching the battlefield because of Allied air action against the bridges over the Loire and other avenues to the front. Rommel had been proved right on two counts; he had nominated the invasion site and forecast the disruptive role of Allied air power.

Disillusion set in quickly. While Rommel reported factually and without drama, his notes were rife with pessimism, highlighting the powerless nature of his position and his inability to do anything to retrieve the advantage. He cited the numerical superiority of his opponents' armour, that supplies were not reaching his men, and that the Luftwaffe was not able to combat the Allied airborne drops of extra men and weaponry. By now he and von Rundstedt were in accord and, in private conversations with colleagues, had quoted a settlement as being Hitler's only way out from the current position.

At the end of June the two men were called to Berchtesgaden to hear Hitler call for a mobile war to be avoided at all costs and insisting that guerrilla actions must be pursued to erode the growing Allied confidence. The Führer claimed that the German fighting spirit had been too weak and of a poor general standard so the German war hero was left to return to his headquarters full of spite and appalled by his treatment. From the later stages of his stay in Africa and his meetings with

Rommel on a tour of inspection of the Atlantic Wall.

the Führer during his trips back from there at that time, Rommel had come to fear the manic side of his leader's mind and his ignorance of the true state of the war. Now he was utterly convinced that Hitler was driven by personal rather than national motives, a belief that eroded what cement continued to commit him to his country's war effort.

Rommel's Last Day at War

Some six weeks after the Allies landed Rommel was making a tour of the German front by car. It was a daily task as it had been for almost every day when he had been on the battlefield and sent his men to war. By now any German road traffic – travelling to or from the front – was a prime target for the pervasive Allied fighter aircraft. The pilots had now become expert at spotting the dust from vehicles travelling over the dry roads and lanes and all such movement was risky.

After spending some time at the headquarters of Sepp Dietrich on 17 July, Erwin Rommel began the journey back to the HQ of Army Group B to get news of fresh enemy incursions. Dietrich reportedly offered a small Volkswagen 'Beetle' for the trip, believing it would be less conspicuous, but it was his Horch staff car that was to carry Rommel on this fateful trip.

Rommel with SS Gruppenführer Sepp Dietrich in northern France, contemplating the inevitable Allied invasion.

It was a particularly nerve-wracking journey; the road was strewn with burning trucks and cars and cluttered with refugees from Normandy and the car was often forced to take minor roads or seek the cover of trees. The party consisted of Rommel, Major Neuhaus, Captain Lang, Daniel – Rommel's regular driver – and Feldwebel Holke, an aircraft lookout. Weaving his way slowly between the damaged traffic, Daniel was encouraged to regain the main road so as to get the Field Marshal back to his HQ as quickly as possible.

On this wider road, the N179 from Livarot to Vimoutiers and, ironically, close to the village of Ste-Foy-de-Montgommery, two aircraft flew low to attack the vehicle. The driver increased speed and headed for the next turning on to a minor road but it was too late. A cannon-shell from the first aircraft shattered the driver's left arm, Rommel was struck in the face by flying glass and, as the driver lost control, was thrown against the side of the car and sustained a triple skull fracture. Colliding with roadside trees, the car was thrown from one side of the road to the other and Rommel, clutching the door handle, was eventually thrown out and lay unconscious in the road. The driver and the major – the latter with a fractured pelvis – were able to scramble out and take shelter, but the Field Marshal remained motionless among the wreckage. Captain Lang was also injured, though less severely, and Holke had survived unscathed.

After Rommel was found to be still alive there was a lengthy delay until another car was able to take the three injured men to hospital. There it was made clear that the Field Marshal would not survive without more sophisticated medical attention and this was only possible a few days later when he could be moved. He had lost huge amounts of blood from head wounds and the initial medical attention – from a local doctor in Livarot – had been barely more than basic first aid.

The hospital, at Bernay some twenty-five miles from the scene of the attack, could not save the driver, but assessed Rommel, with multiple head fractures, a damaged left eye, other injuries caused by flying glass and severe concussion, as having an outside chance of recovery. Attending the Field Marshal was Professor Esch, the Luftwaffe's most talented neurological surgeon, who immediately stressed how remarkable it was that the patient had survived at all. One week after the incident the great man, still unable to open his left eye and suffering deafness in his left ear, was moved to a large hospital outside Paris and, while there, wrote his first letter to his wife in which he, significantly, expressed astonishment about the attempt on the life of the Führer. Even more interesting is that he received, the same day, a telegram of concern and best wishes from Hitler, though we cannot be sure whether the sender had already received the testimony from the plotters that so dangerously spoke of Rommel as one of their number.

The very air power he had warned would render defence against the Allied invasion useless had brought the hero of Caporetto, the fall of France and the North African desert near to death; it had certainly ended his fighting career.

THE GREATEST VICTORY

There are several events in Rommel's career that historians believe merit the description of his greatest victory; this of course, is the case for many high-ranking war generals, certainly many of those who are candidates for inclusion in this series of *Commanders in Focus*. The selection for Erwin Rommel could be drawn from:

Caporetto – the battle that must have given the man and his superiors such confidence and was so full of audacious moves for an officer in his first major experience of action.

The Attack into France – this first test of the Blitzkrieg strategy needed commanders committed to its aims and ambitions, and convinced of its potential. Rommel was entirely in tune with it and employed it masterfully.

The Turnaround in the Desert – though benefiting from the British being side-tracked by the threat to Greece, Rommel made an immediate impact in North Africa and proved himself a master of the use of powerful tanks and anti-tank weaponry in, to him and his men, a new, open battlefield.

Kasserine and Mareth – while these battles were relatively minor and conducted by Rommel when he was ill and destined for defeat in North Africa, they demonstrated the man had lost none of his daring, little of his battlefield acumen, and suggest yet again that given greater support he would have got closer to achieving his goals on the African continent.

Considering the diverse claims of each of the above, and other incidents in his career, we shall study the period 26 May–21 June when, at the battle of the Gazala–Bir Hacheim Line, Rommel put on a brilliant display of armoured force leadership, deploying his 88mm guns in concert with astutely directed infantry and tank attacks. It must be remembered too that this battle came just a few months after his forces had been driven into retreat at a result of Operation 'Crusader', though it was fought against a fresh Allied line created by Rommel's surprise counter in January when he pressured the enemy into withdrawing to this Gazala position. In the interim both sides gathered their thoughts, their men and *matériel* – both were in desperate need of re-supply of the latter – and prepared to take the initiative of the next attack.

The Situation in the Spring of 1942

What Adolf Hitler had really expected of Erwin Rommel when he chose to send him to North Africa we shall never know. If he imagined the region could become a major asset for the Axis powers, a point from which he could gain power and influence all around the Mediterranean and beyond via control of the Suez Canal, these ambitions were sidelined by the spring of 1942 for, by then, all his concentration was focused on his Russian offensive. Whatever he had once wanted or expected his 'Desert Fox' to achieve south of the

Mediterranean, this theatre was now almost a side-show, that would have to look after itself to a very large degree. He had to leave the region to one of his finest generals and his Afrika Korps to scrape for whatever they could get alongside Italian allies who, even under Rommel, were proving to be a military force of limited consequence.

In the light of these circumstances, Rommel's performance at Gazala was remarkable. Of all the land battles of the war, this was one of only a handful where the performance of one of the combatants was executed with such purpose, pace and success that it made headlines around the world, far beyond its own area and the homelands of those involved. Few, if indeed more than one, of the top-performing generals in the 1939–45 conflict would have dreamt of doing what Rommel did – his own generals were not impressed with his plan – and none would have achieved even a portion of his success. Gazala was, in the words of David Chandler, 'a virtuoso performance by Rommel ... and the omens looked ill for the future of the Eighth Army'.[11]

It should be remembered that at this point in the Desert War German High Command was at its most indecisive and confused. Adolf Hitler was thinking only of the Eastern Front and had his leading strategists busily planning a summer offensive there. Indeed, when Rommel flew to OKH Headquarters in March he found no one had the time or inclination to talk of North Africa, and even its possible role in creating an area of control far round the Eastern Mediterranean and beyond did not excite the top table. He was disillusioned by this lack of support, complaining, 'They did not realise that with relatively small means we could have won victories in the Near East ... ahead of us lay territories containing an enormous wealth of raw materials ... which could have freed us of all our anxieties about oil ... it was obvious that the opinion of High Command had not changed from that which they had expressed in 1941, namely that Africa was a "lost cause".'

This was not an entirely accurate assessment and contained the bias of understandable bitterness. Russia was the big theme, that was certain, but Hitler was never likely to stop dreaming and there was a distant aim to use North Africa as a route for gaining territory and influence all around the Middle East and north through the lands of the Arabian Gulf, the old Ottoman Empire and up to the Black Sea. What the Führer certainly did not want to see was this theatre becoming the drain on resources that, with the Allied control of the Mediterranean Sea and skies, and the vital base of Malta, it was appearing to be. Every vessel sunk *en route* to North African ports, every aircraft lost to Allied planes and ships, was a dagger in the heart of the German military manufacturing industries which were striving to keep the Führer active on his many fronts.

Certainly Malta was often in Rommel's mind. One look at the geography of the Mediterranean suggested that the central sector could surely be controlled by military occupation of the islands of Sicily and Sardinia; in theory it was ludicrous to believe that the tiny speck of Malta could have a significant role ... it was too small, too susceptible. The first two were Italian possessions and Rommel must have often looked down on Sicily as he flew from Rome and wondered why Malta, a minor outcrop off its south-eastern tip, could possibly be such a thorn in his side. He was constantly thrown into despair as more supplies reached the enemy via the tiny island base and men and *matériel* bound for him were lost to Allied air and sea strikes. It was only on the infrequent occasions when German air strikes caused enough damage to interrupt Allied aerial activity that more supplies reach his forces. It may seem perplexing that Hitler never committed himself to capturing Malta, but the fact is that when the time was most opportune to do so, Egypt was seen as the bigger and more necessary prize, and Rommel eventually agreed.

Most historians would contend that this was a strategic error. Rommel found throughout the North African campaign that he was constantly held back by the supply situation, and, it must be added, his own speed of attack. With Malta so close to defeat on more than one occasion it might have been expected that time would have been found to complete the job and help reduce the threat of Allied air and sea attacks and, by definition, improve the supply situation to the Axis forces. Kesselring complained that the failure to complete the capture of the

A German supply convoy moves across the North African landscape. Rommel never received sufficient armour or fuel at the levels he needed to secure victory.

island lost the Germans the war in North Africa; few could deny it was a major contributory cause.

There had been a comprehensive plan to invade Malta with paratroops, airfield bombing and naval attacks, but it was never implemented. Indeed, it was nearly the case that the British spent so much time and energy protecting the island that they actually appeared to give this priority over the army they were so well positioned to supply. For all the while Rommel was so desperately short of supplies, the Allies were fighting to save Malta as well as battling the 'Desert Fox'.

This prepares us to look at the situation on the Gazala defence line in the early spring of 1942. Auchinleck had been instructed by his masters in London that he should look to attack the enemy as soon as possible, ideally during May, since all believed that Rommel would not be ready for offensive action until at least June, but would be sure to mount an attack as soon as he could. Thus it was that the Eighth Army was deployed in attacking mode along the line between Gazala and Bir Hacheim, a distance of some 45 miles, with huge fuel and supply dumps close to their lines. It is ironic that Rommel was so prone to advance beyond the point where he could keep his men supplied, whereas, here, the Allies were so committed to attacking with good sources of supply that the closeness of them actually hindered their withdrawal when it came.

As we have established, the Gazala line consisted of a series of wired and mined 'boxes' between which were large gaps in which narrow minefields were sparsely patrolled. The concentration of the boxes was in the north where the three South African Brigades plus 151 and 69 Brigades were positioned in their temporary fortified pens; there was then a six-mile gap to 150 Brigade just west of Sidi Muftah and a further thirteen miles to the Free French unit in their 'box' at Bir Hacheim. It was not a line and to call it so was, as Ronald Lewin puts it, 'a grave mistake, because such words soon begin to stand for something real'.[12] And it certainly was not designed for defence, but as a point from which an advance could be effectively mounted.

For Rommel it was always a question of how soon to attack and what tactics he would use. No Allied – and probably no German – commander would have chosen to attack when Rommel did. He had received a large convoy of tanks in February and was intent on using them … and this time he was planning hard, so hard that he was not ready to attack until May.

While the 'Gazala Line' was being prepared Auchinleck was being constantly bombarded, from London! Churchill was under pressure to cancel out the Axis threat in North Africa and regularly passed on that urgency to Auchinleck. The latter knew it would be foolish to commit himself to offensive action until he, like Rommel, secured more tanks and long-lasting superiority in the air. He was able to convince Churchill's emissaries, Sir Stafford Cripps and General Nye, of this when they flew out to Cairo to confront him, and it was there agreed that Auchinleck would begin the offensive no later than the middle of June, by which time he would have more American tanks.

From the moment he saw the line the Allies had prepared, Rommel was clear in his mind that the best way of attacking it would be to ignore it and sweep round its southern end. This was the longest route to the ultimate goal of Tobruk, but, that fact apart, it was the best of all the options he considered. It was a strategy as old as time; all defensive lines are, potentially, strongest at their centre and weakest at their extremities and it is a long practised military art to extend the defensive line at either end or both so that its resources become stretched and thus create weak points. Here, with a freshly supplied mobile force, Rommel felt he had no need to work to weaken the line, he would simply drive round it. In *The Rommel Papers*, the Swabian states his admiration for the complex work that had gone into creating the Allied line at Gazala, but castigates its basic weakness of having an open flank that could be circumnavigated.

By choosing this option he used his every advantage. If he drove at the northerly (sea) end of the line, or at its centre, he would be conducting the battle as the opposition had expected and wanted, would need to expend great effort and resources to achieve success and would be failing to use his best asset to its maximum advantage. His newly arrived tanks could, he believed, spearhead a drive around the line, head due north to Tobruk and do so with pace, power, and, initially at least, little resistance. Although the scheme seemed wise to Rommel, its choice alarmed his own generals and was contrary to what the enemy anticipated. Auchinleck was expecting Rommel to use the directly opposite tactic, to feint to the south and commit a full drive against the centre.

So convinced was 'the Auk' that he was reading his opponent's intentions correctly that, only hours before the initial Axis moves, he was urging General Ritchie to mass his tanks at the centre of the line. Ritchie, to be fair, was not as convinced as his superior and let it be known that he considered Rommel might arc around below Bir Hacheim, though other generals felt an attack nearer to the coast was more probable. This divergence of opinion was damaging now and later, and the direct opposite of the situation obtaining in Axis HQ where what alternative views there may have been, and even when they were voiced, were not allowed to damage the standing of the top man. Once Rommel made a decision his generals followed instructions to the letter, without hesitation or dispute.

Another aspect of Rommel's generalship was the clarity of instructions when given. He seldom issued a complicated remit, preferring to maintain momentum and confidence with clear and succinct orders. But then he was always so close to the front that he could amend the instructions as he went along. There was never any doubt in the minds of those receiving his orders that he was entirely committed to them himself, and expected his men to be; the orders never spoke of 'if' and 'maybe' but of actual aims and intentions and, as mentioned, seldom referred to anything beyond the immediate target.

Rommel Attacks

The orders for the Axis attack were issued on 20 May. Their forces were basically divided into two sectors with, facing the centre of the Allied line, the mobile forces of the Italian XX Corps, the Afrika Korps and 90th Light Division; and north of the 150 Brigade box, the Italian X and XXI Infantry Corps, some German infantry and much of the artillery units. Late in the afternoon of 26 May, Rommel moved his mobile forces forwards along the line of the Trigh Capuzzo in the direction of the 150 Brigade box. It seemed Auchinleck had been right, the 'Desert Fox' was determined to test himself against a strong point of the Allied line.

As darkness fell, however, the route was changed and Rommel, leading the first group, suddenly veered south and headed for the Line's open flank of which he was so critical. It was if a dam had been built only 95 per cent across the width of a valley – but remember, this was a line the Allies had expected to attack from, not to defend. The stream of Axis infantry was now rushing towards the gap.

Shortly after the change of direction, Rommel detached the Trieste Division of the Italian XXI Corps to move due east again with the purpose of attacking the minefield line below 150 Brigade and so opening a supply route in addition to the

BATTLE OF GAZALA, 26 MAY TO 13 JUNE 1942

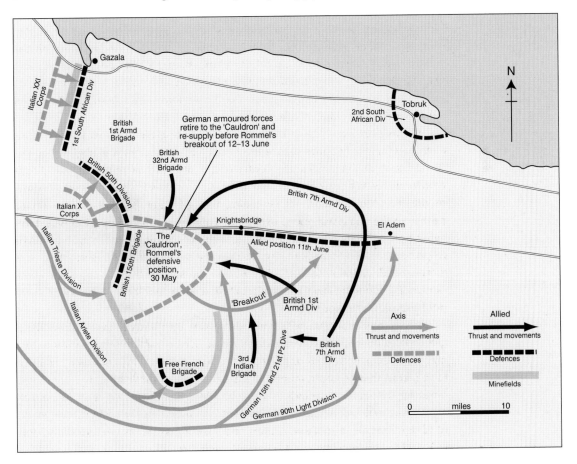

one he expected to create via Bir Hacheim. Now, with the units in the north moving on the South Africans north of Alam Hamza, the 'boxes' of 69 and 151 Brigades, and the northern edge of the 150 Brigade position adjacent to the Trigh Capuzzo, all Rommel had to ensure was the successful capture of Bir Hacheim in order to be able to turn the Afrika Korps northwards.

But in a late change of plan, the German had decided to have the Ariete Division take Bir Hacheim, rather than the Afrika Korps. Whether this was a considered policy shift because he was sure the Italians could account for the limited defences of the Free French, or simply his impatience to get on with, and spearhead, the turn to the north and the ultimate goal of Tobruk, we shall never know, but it was an error. At the time he could see how easily his forces accounted for Indian 3 Motorised Brigade just south of Bir Hacheim, and within hours was hearing of 90th Division catching 7 Motorised Brigade by surprise. He must have been a confident man at this point.

Then came the reversals. The German, by his own admission, had underestimated the strength of the British Armoured Divisions, especially their fresh firepower represented by the new American Grant tanks of whose presence until now he had been unaware. Additionally, the Italians were not enjoying great success; Ariete was losing many tanks and still failing to take Bir Hacheim, and Trieste had not yet been able to get through the minefields to the north. On top of this he was unable to establish the progress of 90th Light Division, and the intended diversionary attacks on the north of the line had not made much progress.

Although the Allies had most certainly been caught by surprise by the nature and width of the Axis advance, and were in many instances slow to react, they soon began to harry the attackers who, in their quest for speed had lost their formation in places. If the Allied commanders could hold the 150 Brigade 'box' and deploy 22 Armoured Brigade and 2nd Armoured Division against Rommel's forward units, they could stunt the Axis ambitions almost before they revealed themselves. With the setbacks among the Italian Divisions, the battle had quickly swung against Rommel, for until Bir Hacheim had been taken his longer supply route could not function, and unless the Trieste Division could get through 150 Brigade the added benefit of a shorter access route would also be lost. Such is war; Rommel had lurched from euphoria to despair within hours. By midday on 27 May, the German was close to throwing in the towel. The 15th Panzer Division alone had lost 100 tanks and crucial elements of his scheme had gone awry. If he continued his push towards Tobruk without the certainty of supply routes through the Allied line he would be putting his entire force at risk.

The Vital Decision

Although Rommel had continued his push north towards Tobruk, he was halted south of the Sidra Ridge and Trigh Capuzzo. All around him his tanks were being lost at an alarming rate: the Ariete Division seeing many destroyed in their attempt to take Bir Hacheim, Trieste looked likely to suffer the same fate if it could not quickly complete its break through the minefields, and the German divisions being equally battered by the new Allied tank strength. He still felt he had the advantage of fighting a planned action whereas his opponents were clearly reacting piecemeal to each of his thrusts, but, despite the tactics of the

Rommel and his staff in discussion.

Allied armoured brigades being in his own words, 'incomprehensible', the German could not pursue his own detailed strategy if significant elements of it – ammunition and fuel supplies – had not yet been secured.

In his decision to keep driving north Rommel was surely being propelled by his desire to capture Tobruk and his belief that, despite their acquisition of new tanks, the enemy was using them inefficiently and would continue to do so if pressured into ill-considered moves. He sensed, as did his senior officers, that the Allied commanders had, as intended, been caught planning for their own offensive and had no cohesive scheme for defence. If they could not coordinate an organised and substantial riposte the German stood a chance of reaching his objective.

Rommel's plan for the battle was, in David Chandler's words, 'bold and full of risks; its execution was destined to be brilliant, but not without grave crises'. He had already seen his forces overcome two motorised brigades, capture Retma, swamp 4 Armoured Brigade and threaten 22 Armoured Brigade within the first day and a half of the offensive, but by 29 May he was having to head back personally towards Bir Hacheim in order to supervise the unblocking of his supply columns there. He was driven by the adrenalin rush of battle, but still weakened by his poor health so to undertake this difficult task personally, at times in ferocious sandstorms that were testing many younger men, is a testament to his great determination.

Perhaps wearied by his efforts of the day and still concerned at the steady depletion of his tank force, the 'Desert Fox' suddenly implemented a complete change of strategy. In a masterful mid-battle tactical switch he turned his armour west again and created his own 'box' butting up to the Allied line north of Trigh el Abd to a point close by Sidra Ridge. The 'box,' actually more of a rough semi-circle and a creation that was to become known as 'The Cauldron', enveloped the 150 Brigade 'box' and was surrounded by a ring of guns. By extending it to the Allied lines, Rommel secured himself the chance to create a broad path through the minefield to build the shorter supply route he needed to move on again when the chance arose.

This move dumbfounded his opponents. While they were now more certain than ever that the 'Fox' was heading for Tobruk, they could not comprehend this major pause and re-grouping – it was so unlike the attack-minded German. Ritchie, the Allied commander, was in a quandary for he might have dreamt of having the Axis forces all in one place, albeit it a defended one, and had he set up the situation by dint of his own efforts he would have surely attacked. But the German battlefield master had shaken Neil Ritchie's predecessors with his cunning; the British officer hesitated.

By the time the Allies were stirred to attack, on 5 June, it was weak and bereft of clear planning. Its failure saw the Allied tank losses almost double since Rommel's initiative and it prompted the German to look to complete the disintegration of the Allied line by sending a new force south in an attempt finally to secure Bir Hacheim. Once this had been achieved the next Axis moves could be activated and this was to be on 11 June.

Breakout from 'The Cauldron'

Rommel still had forces facing the South African and British Divisions forming the northernmost sector of the Line just west of Gazala, and was of the opinion that Auchinleck and Ritchie would not dare to move those defenders while that confrontation was in place. He had overrun 150 Brigade during the formation of 'The Cauldron', despite the very best defensive spirit being shown by that formation, and repulsed attempts by XIII Corps to relieve it, so he believed that he had removed much of the opposition that a move out of his defensive position and towards Tobruk would encounter.

The Allied efforts to challenge Rommel's defensive positions were little more than ordinary. During the night of 4 June, XXX Corps was set to move infantry forward across the Aslagh Ridge while XIII Corps approached in the direction of Sidra Ridge, with tank formations to follow, but inexperienced troops, poorly armed with inferior anti-tank weaponry, moved too slowly across the open desert plain. Auchinleck acknowledged the dismal failure of the operation – code-named 'Aberdeen' – and considered it the turning-point of the battle, but, if truth be told, it would have been better not to mount an operation against 'The Cauldron' than attempt this weak and poorly co-ordinated move.

Rommel had shown a new element of his strategic intellect by his creation of 'The Cauldron'. He knew what he had to do to hold it and believed it would be so threatening a position, and yet apparently vulnerable enough, as to encourage Allied response, and so it was. Once he assessed the manner of the Allied attacks he was confident that they would not be successful; he also saw the enemy expending its limited resources on a worthless exercise. In one respect Auchinleck was right, Operation 'Aberdeen' was the decisive moment in the Gazala battle, but he was failing to acknowledge the wily battlefield skill of his adversary; the failure of 'Aberdeen' was as much down to Rommel's drawing the enemy on to him and setting the parameters of the contest as it was to the inadequacy of the Allied planning and execution.

The German move, when it came, was not along the shortest route towards the fortified port. His main force did not sweep out to the north-east across Sidra Ridge, though 21st Panzer Division and Ariete did feint a move that way, but south and then east in the direction of El Adem. Although this divided up his manpower it did bring immediate results and within 24 hours he had achieved a good degree of dominance over the Allied forces. To Ritchie the enemy seemed to be everywhere; he found himself unable to focus on any one point for whatever counter he might conceive. Now out of the confines of his defensive position, where he had contentedly sat for days, the 'Desert Fox' was on the rampage again, back to his old form; just a week before he had been in the depths of despair as his attack on the Gazala–Bir Hacheim line had faltered badly.

The scant protection for infantry moving across open desert is evident here. These Allied troops have scraped shallow shelters, surrounded by burning enemy vehicles.

Erwin Rommel, ever the quick thinker on the open battlefield, was in his element. Allied commanders became confused and disorientated as they sought to effect concerted action, as the German set 15th Panzer on 2nd Armoured Division and 4 Armoured Brigade from their south, while 21st Panzer Division raced out of its position to harry them from the west. It was a devastating pincer movement that all but removed the Allied threat to his progress towards Tobruk. The German now had the important prize of the port in his sights, but he could also cut off the Allied forces to the north of their line and he was back to his best here, dashing around the battle-zone,

encouraging his men, re-directing their efforts and keeping in touch with any problems and setbacks they were encountering. For the moment he was more concerned about the continued air superiority of the enemy and the damage it was inflicting on his formations.

The Scots Guards abandoned their small Knightsbridge 'box' on 13 June, reluctantly moving north overnight. Rommel was highly complimentary about 201 Guards Brigade, citing their courage and tenacity, but their removal from this central point was another blow for Ritchie as he sought to repair the now gaping holes in his defensive positions. But it was a lost cause because Rommel,

by dint of his recent progress, now had twice as many tanks as the opposition despite the fact that he had lost more than he had anticipated.

The Main Prize

Having lusted after Tobruk from the very beginning, the 'Desert Fox' was at last within sight of the port. Once in his hands, Kesselring and others responsible for getting supplies of men and equipment to the theatre would have no excuse; the availability of the Libyan town might even encourage Hitler to allocate more resources.

In Cairo and London there were hurried but extensive discussions on what the Allies could do in the face of Rommel's imminent attack. Churchill's view was that Tobruk should never be given up; he cited the occasions when Rommel's fortunes had been at a low ebb and how he remained under-sourced and vulnerable. Auchinleck was reluctant to leave any troops behind to fight a losing battle; if the port was to be evacuated, he felt they should withdraw so as to be able to fight another day. In any event, the more optimistic Allied opinion was that Rommel's probable occupation of Tobruk would be temporary.

The attack on Tobruk came from the south-east on 20 June and for once it was German air attacks that led the way. Dive-bombers pummelled the remaining defences and enabled elements of the Afrika Korps to navigate the perimeter defence without difficulty and reach the minefields three miles beyond by midday. The airfields a further five miles forward were in Axis hands shortly afterwards and by early evening 21st Panzer Division rolled into the port itself. By the following morning all resistance had been quelled and General Klopper, the South African commanding the garrison at this time, surrendered. There had been times during recent months when Rommel felt he might

A posed photograph showing men of the Australian 20th Brigade's 2/13th Infantry Battalion poised to enter Tobruk through wire barriers.

never take Tobruk and seldom had he believed the task, if and when it came, would be so trouble-free.

The Eighth Army had been humbled. The Commonwealth troops had been reduced to a haphazard, bedraggled force that, through inexperienced and inadequate command, had been rendered ineffective by a supreme battlefield genius who, let it be remembered, had been humiliated himself just a few months before.

This is why Gazala was such a triumph for Erwin Rommel. When he was licking his wounds near El Agheila in January, few would have predicted that the German would be able to mount such an audacious attack as was seen here. By the end of that month two-thirds of the Axis armies had been destroyed, with the vital Afrika Korps forces reduced by half. Morale was low, the Italians were at their lowest ebb following their trudge back from the Libyan port after their work there was abandoned. Rommel had lost an alarming 93 per cent of his tanks and 80 per cent of his aircraft. Surely no commander has ever recovered from such a sorry state to win a major action against all odds within such a short time.

Inferior in respect of supply networks, air support and effective allies in battle, the sickly 'Desert Fox' worked against the odds month after month. From a situation of disadvantage he had achieved dramatic success, aided by the Allies whose leadership seemed incapable of exploiting the superior benefits they enjoyed including, of late, a numerical superiority in armour. Confused and nervous when Rommel delayed his push for Tobruk and 'imprisoned' himself in the defensive 'Cauldron', they still failed to wrest the initiative and all this had degenerated from a point where they had chosen the site of their line at Gazala and been planning their own offensive. Rommel won the battle from a position where most, if not all, of the odds were against him.

The surrender of 35,000 Allied troops and a grand haul of diverse supplies, including 1,400 tons of fuel, was a justified prize for so supreme an effort, but, when all came to be assessed, the great achievement here did not win the Desert War nor even secure the port for long; it was back in Allied hands by mid-November as the defeated Rommel fled past it on his sorry retreat after El Alamein.

A jubilant Erwin Rommel luxuriated in his success as recognition of his work arrived from Hitler by means of a notice announcing the Swabian's promotion to Field Marshal. In London an opposite mood was leading to a vote of censure against Churchill in the House of Commons, demonstrating the remarkable impact of the fall of Tobruk and the total crisis now facing the Eighth Army. Using his bonus quantities of fuel Rommel typically chose not to rest on his laurels but immediately set off to the Egyptian border and on to Mersa Matruh.

The disjointed command skills of Neil Ritchie saw Auchinleck arrive to take control himself. The Allies had been shaken to the core by a three-weeks' campaign by Erwin Rommel during which he had outthought and outfought them from a situation where most generals would have chosen not to attack at all. His readiness to adapt his tactics as the situation demanded showed the resourcefulness and enterprise that the more stolid Allied commanders lacked. The lauded Eighth Army was in a parlous state and Allied strategy in North Africa required to be completely re-thought.

4

ROMMEL AS A MILITARY COMMANDER

There was nothing overly complicated about Erwin Rommel as a military commander, though dozens of books have spent a million words endeavouring to make it seem so.

Three features, when combined, set him aside from most others as a military commander. First, he was always in favour of action; to him an idle commander or a static battleground was wasteful. Secondly, he commonly led from the front, not just *closer* to the front-line than other generals but genuinely *at* the front. Thirdly, as if in contradiction, he was not a reckless, glory-seeking cavalier, as one might expect in someone with the first two characteristics. He was always ready to set an example to his officers and men and in war no one can ask more of his superior than that they train and inspire in a practical manner and are prepared to share the setbacks and the tough challenges. It is the same in any walk of life.

Although some would classify these traits as potential faults, signs of irresponsibility or a failure to understand the need to protect the senior man in any situation, most historians accept that it is these that made Rommel a very special commander. From his earliest commands he won respect and admiration from his men and, though this was brought about by far more than simply setting an example, the fact that he was prepared to go where he was sending his forces and to confront the same risks he was asking them to take, led to a loyalty that was tangible and beyond measurable value.

It has been suggested that Erwin Rommel was not an innovator, but simply a resourceful implementor of other people's strategies and, to some degree, this is correct. Guderian was capable of more original theoretical thinking, and still a fine battlefield commander. But few have ever mastered the command of a fluid military situation better than Rommel for, whatever prerequisites you set for such work, this man would meet them.

We have established that Rommel's early military career did not see him displaying the maverick tendencies he was to show later, so what was it that changed his manner and his methods? There is every likelihood that part of the change was down to a maturing mind and the greater confidence that comes with stability within an adult environment. Even so, it appears that he was blessed with the sub-conscious attribute that he could apply his basic principles of life to every situation in which he found himself.

It was already apparent that the static, mind-numbing boredom of the Western Front was not going to suit the young Rommel though, again, his childhood had not suggested a quest for a life of action as opposed to a less physically strenuous existence. It surely benefited his career that he was neither ensnared in the static warfare of the Western Front or, in the 1939–45 conflict, sent to Russia. In these locations it is questionable whether the attributes quoted above would have so flourished and been fully utilised, especially since they would not have afforded the same degree of autonomy and freedom of command he was to enjoy elsewhere. In North Africa in particular, he was not bordered by other huge Army Groups as he dashed around the desert, nor did he spend much time in the slow-moving Italian Campaign, though it would have been interesting to see him let loose there.

During the Great War it was small-scale actions, often at night and in unfavourable terrain, that brought out the best in him. The conditions he encountered in such work enabled him to lead all his men by example, they could *all* see that he was prepared to put himself in the line of fire, to make the one vital move that would win the day. The inter-war years saw him studying the theories of war and how new weaponry could change grand battlefield strategies, but someone must have considered using a man with his 1914–18 record to evolve new practices and possibilities for special purpose and small-unit warfare. Had this happened one can surmise that clandestine battle-zone activity would have been much more prevalent than it was; perhaps Rommel would have been Germany's David Stirling.

When in 1940 he adapted to Blitzkrieg and, later in the desert, to broad battle areas and the large-scale deployment of combined tank and artillery power, it

Rommel had fought against the Italians during World War I but, as allies in the desert, found their performance mediocre.

was a challenge for which he could not draw on personal, practical experience. Simply, he had to show adaptability, and did so with mighty success, applying his basic tenets for soldiering success to whatever test he faced, and he with greater success than most. This is what set him apart; where others had their specialities, Rommel was the man for all occasions; few men who reached his level of command ended their career with such a diverse list of achievements obtained from so mixed a set of military actions.

Until Hitler gave Rommel his wish of a Panzer command, the man had not fought with tanks. Presumably the Führer did not look upon this as too great a gamble for he knew of the Swabian's diligent theoretical work at the War Colleges and we know he had read his man's best-selling account of his infantry action. Perhaps he actually foresaw that the talents his man had shown in the 1914–18 War could dovetail perfectly into the Blitzkrieg philosophy. If he did, he was right!

Just as he had reacted promptly and positively to each new challenge he had faced a quarter of a century before, Rommel wasted no time in mastering his new remit. This may have been the easiest time to become accustomed to leading a tank- and artillery-based formation because Blitzkrieg was unleashed against an unsuspecting and confused enemy who had nothing – weaponry or strategy – to oppose it with. He still showed, however, acute understanding of the fundamentals of the strategy, and employed them with ruthlessness and cunning; not a talent that a good number of the German officers who had worked with the few tanks in the Great War were able to show.

Rommel with his artillery commander, Lieutenant-General Karl Böttcher (left).

It is here that those who argue that Blitzkrieg was a philosophy more than it was a strategy gain ground. Improved tank technology, more efficient communication processes, and faster, more potent aircraft were the background of the tactic, but even these assets were not a winning formula in every instance. The glue that sealed the elements into a formidable whole was the commander charged with deploying it. In Rommel's work in Belgium, France and the Desert, we have a sense of his assessing how the bold new strategy could help him achieve the goals he had been set. There is a subtle difference between this and a commander following a battle plan he perceives as having been created by the strategy. The racing car breaks a lap record not only by the great speed it provides to the driver but by how the driver uses that power to complete the circuit the way he believes to be best.

It is always fascinating to chart how a general's early career influences his later commands. There are those who change their thinking the moment they taste the power of command, and those who retain an empathy with the men of lower ranks. Others have been seen to struggle with advances in the science and technology of the battleground. Napoleon used his soldiering achievements to secure national status and power, and was perhaps too ready to apply military practices to political office. Others such as Churchill and, to a degree, Eisenhower, found their command experiences or leadership qualities to be of value in their later careers. Most change their thinking as their responsibilities alter, becoming more formal, less concerned with the weaponry itself than how it might be deployed.

Erwin Rommel barely amended his battlefield philosophy from the moment of his first action in the murky environs of Bleid. This was a military commander who remembered how and why he fought his first battle, how seriously he should treat his men, why imagination and quick-thinking were as valuable in Blitzkrieg conditions as they were when leading a small mountain troop. This was not intransigence but a conviction that certain basic beliefs hold fast whatever the circumstances; in the case of Rommel it was a demonstration of a military commander working with a broader canvas rather than the narrower one some accuse him of. His attitudes to military command may have been based on simplicity – they were not simplistic!

For the German drive into France, von Manstein chose the Ardennes as a principal route – as Hitler would again in December 1944. Guderian's memoirs suggest that only he, with von Manstein and Hitler himself, believed the scheme would work, but we also know that Rommel, supportive of German national strength and independence rather than of the specific Nazi cause, approved of the audacity being shown and was thrilled to be part of it. His work between the wars had convinced him that the tank was the future of warfare. His belief in pace around the battlefield, of hitting the opponent hard in his centre and around his flanks, was made more achievable by these machines that were apparently impenetrable by bayonet, bullet or bombardment.

Although close to fifty and still suffering from poor health, including the injuries of the earlier war, Rommel had retained his youthful vitality and eagerness to be tested in combat. Now he was determined to make the best he could of his first Blitzkrieg command, but he was quickly appalled by the attitude of the enemy – just as he had been with some of his Italian foes those years before. 'We opened fire, the French retreated,' he moaned, as if to show he expected every warrior to have his ambition and determination.

The thrust across Belgium and France was made for this man, but, as we have considered elsewhere, he did not perform so well because of weak opposition. Although he was indeed guilty of an error on the one occasion his progress was seriously tested, at Arras, Rommel accomplished the moves required of him with greater effectiveness than any of his colleagues. If he had a weakness as a military commander it was his somewhat ambivalent attitude towards supply logistics, and he moved too fast for his supply chain on this occasion, but he was constantly surprising his fellow officers with the pace of his forward movement which rendered day-old logistical solutions obsolete.

He quickly recognised the North African desert to be an entirely different war. In his race across Belgium and France – crossing valleys and hills, rivers and gorges, with towns and forests to pass around or through – the use of the tank was hindered to the point where the air-support element of the Blitzkrieg tactic was fundamental and, at times, progress was made by old-fashioned leg work. In the desert he was able to fight a true tank versus tank war with artillery barrages and the battle scene was seldom static. The most mobile won the day – it was a perfect scenario for the fast-thinking Swabian.

There is no doubt that Rommel was quicker than the Allied commanders to appreciate the type of warfare that would bring success in Africa. Although Wavell had enjoyed great success against the Italians, it was not achieved through new tactics but more the standard of the opposition. Rommel quickly learned that motorised armour effectively deployed was infinitely preferable to non-motorised infantry however well they might seek to defend themselves. Only a fortification in the style of Tobruk could neutralise fast-moving and potent tank formations.

Just as forward and flanking movements could be so easily accomplished and effective on the open plains of North Africa, so withdrawals by any other means than well-organised and equipped mobile forces was tantamount to creating carnage. Rommel knew this well and suffered the embarrassment of it when retreating from Cyrenaica in the winter of 1941 without sufficient tanks and motorised transport.

So Rommel put in place a new form of mobile warfare that relied more on his personal input and direction than the textbooks at War College. It still had at its heart his long-held desire to outflank the enemy so as to attack their rear, and he stated its two basic reasons for seeking envelopment to be – the enemy is placed in the worst tactical situation imaginable, since fire can be brought to bear on him from all sides and even when he is caught only on three sides his position is tactically untenable, and, when the envelopment is completed, he is tactically compelled to evacuate the area he occupies.

He added, however, that he saw that the ownership of motorised power on both sides could mean that the units being surrounded could more easily force their way out of the ring by attacking its weakest point. Thus, he maintained, an encircled force could only be destroyed if bad leadership failed to take any chance to break out, fighting strength had already been weakened, or the units were unable to do so because of lack of motorised transport or fuel.

Rommel's success in the Desert certainly came from his understanding of the primary tactics needed, then the speed with which he often implemented them. Although he was criticised, and still is, for his lack of attention to supply situations, he always stressed that they were a basic tenet for mobile warfare strategy. He always paid attention to protecting his own supplies and to attacking those of the enemy, but, at times, was so concerned to press home an advantage that he led his beloved tanks too far ahead of his fuel stores.

To deploy his tanks effectively, Rommel knew his military Intelligence needed to be extensive and authoritative, and that the information should be forwarded to him at best possible speed. This was cited by him as one of his reasons for remaining so close to the front-line as he wanted to interpret the incoming information and translate it immediately into instructions to his forward tank and artillery commanders. The Intelligence reports received from reconnaissance flights deteriorated for Rommel as the Desert War progressed and German aircraft were increasingly kept from the skies. Also, of course, he eventually suffered from the British cracking the German codes and thus intercepting the signals between German High Command and his HQ.

In his own writings Rommel seeks to attempt to defend his own military philosophy by distinguishing between 'operational and tactical boldness, and a military gamble'. The former, he suggests is one that has some chance of success but, if a failure, leaves the commander with sufficient options to handle the result. The gamble, he opines, is one where the alternative to success is only failure. By this description he never gambled and his boldness often brought success or, if not that, came very close to it or left a retrievable situation.

He had a hatred of compromise and, one suspects, believed that it came about when action was not decisive. The German preferred to weigh the possible results of action rather than compare the value of action against inaction and would prefer to take the grander choice than smaller-scale moves that, in his view, were just as complicated to manage and follow through.

His constant desire for pace and quick reaction was born in his realisation that when war became mobile speed was of the essence. Rapid moves around the battlefield could bring superiority to weaponry that was otherwise of equal power to the opposition, or get your forces and weaponry to a chosen point before the enemy could use it. It was the traditional basis of warfare recoded to the age of the tank and long-range artillery. The need of pace was part of Rommel's training regime, his officers being required to pass on his thinking to those of lower ranks and see that when speed was demanded it could be delivered.

When it came to his fondness for working alongside his men in the front-line, the man who had led from the front from his first live action defended his policy by betraying a certain mistrust of the ability of junior officers to carry out instructions to the letter. One should not assume, he said, that 'every local commander will make as much of a situation as there is to be made out of it'. Because he seemed to have limitless levels of energy he expected others to be able to go without rest and refreshment as he could, and he believed that failure to complete a certain task was often down to reluctance to make the physical effort. Perhaps this is why he would change a wheel, check the mechanics of a tank or even help clear land mines when he was in the front-line and thus demonstrate that there was always work to do if the call to move was to be responded to without delay.

The 'Desert Fox' was not the finest of communicators by the established means, though, in his own notes on command, he rated highly the need to be so. What concerned him most in terms of communication, however, was the need for mechanics to have the best and most up-to-date technical knowledge and all troops to have a clear awareness of what specific instructions meant. He was convinced that soldiers reacted better to a Commander-in-Chief they regularly saw at the front, sharing the dangers that such a policy meant, rather than one who would stay far behind the combat line and issue orders from a distance.

If Rommel is correctly described as a 'soldier's soldier' it is because he never stopped being a simple warrior himself. We have seen he gained command at a reasonably early age, but even thirty years on from that point he was still seeking to marry the roles of command and combat soldier. Although some of his elders would urge a greater caution on him, particularly in North Africa where his capture at certain points could genuinely have lost the campaign, many more had to acknowledge that his astute battle decisions most often came about because he knew what was happening at the front, was entirely aware of what specific weaponry could achieve, had seen the terrain for himself, and, more often than not, was convinced enough of his decision to lead the next move himself. 'The best results', he wrote, 'are obtained by the commander whose ideas develop freely from the conditions around him and have not previously been channelled into any fixed pattern.'

Pattern and orthodoxy was not the route for Erwin Rommel.

During the time he was in a German hospital in the summer of 1942 and again after he left North Africa for good and before he took command of Army Group B, Rommel wrote copious notes and general thoughts about his war experiences to that point. The resulting book, enjoying several translations and best-seller status ever since, is insightful and thorough, seldom self-promotional but often critical of those who adversely affected his potential to achieve greater success.

In the latter category he is regularly critical of Hitler and the German High Command, especially at the time when, in North Africa, he was made well aware that his work was considered a very minor adjunct to the national war effort, at that time mostly concerned with the Eastern Front. He complains about the failure to understand just what success in North Africa could have brought to the German nation in terms of valuable territorial gains and the raw materials they held. His remarks demonstrate that Rommel concerned himself with national achievement while pursuing the war effort in his own theatre.

He is clear in his belief that the poor supply situation that constantly blighted his efforts in the Desert was not insuperable and that, with the right level of resolve, could have been improved to the point where battlefield success followed. He suggests that all that was needed 'was a man with real personality to deal with these questions in Rome' and you know that Rommel was thinking that he, had he been in that position, would have managed to correct the position. He complains that if he had been given a fraction of the men, machines and weapons allocated to the seventy Divisions allocated to the battles for

The port of Benghazi changed hands several times and therefore suffered bombing by both the Allies and the Axis.

France and Italy, he could have forced the Allies out of North Africa. He does not say whether this would have had to be before the 'Torch' landings, but laments the fact that supplies were doubled, all too late, when the Germans were holed up in Tunis.

In commenting on the vastly better supply situation enjoyed by the Allied opposition forces, Rommel cites the period in the spring of 1942 when Kesselring's actions against Malta and an element of control over the Central Mediterranean as the only time when he considered the enemy under the same pressure for supplies as he was. He complains about the difficulties of setting tactical goals when one knew the British had access to fuel from the Near East and could send convoys close to Italian territory without let or hindrance, and one has to feel sympathy for this argument when assessing the quality of Rommel's performance in Africa. In summary he saw the Western Desert as a priority region for one side and a side-show for the other.

The thinking behind Rommel's brilliant tactics at Gazala was to draw the majority of British tanks up behind the centre and northern section of the Allied line. If he could launch a fake advance in this direction so as to stimulate the required move by the Allies, the ground behind the line that he needed to take with his broad sweep around the south of Bir Hacheim would be clearer and his route north-eastwards to Tobruk more open. He had assumed, as part of his plan, that the vital island of Malta would have been captured by then, but realised far too late that the project had been abandoned, causing him to complain bitterly about his scheme to take the island himself being rejected.

In his writings he admits that the early stages of Gazala did not go as planned, but that the tide was turned when he reset the objectives, defended their positions so well and found the dispositions of the Allied forces so poorly conceived. He is pleased to endorse the words of Liddell Hart in criticising the nature of the Allied fighting which the German agrees was full of courage but lacking modern thinking. 'The British Command had not drawn the inferences which it should have drawn from the defeat of 1941–42,' he writes. In other words, he considered himself more innovative and open to change, and at this point he was right.

A photograph taken by Rommel during one of his many reconnaissance flights.

The rules of warfare are constantly changing by the evolution of weaponry and Rommel was well aware of this. Although he had not experienced the static trench warfare of 1914–18, he realised that few of the principles governing that combat were relevant to him in North Africa; he embraced change and was delighted to employ new thinking and see it work. His effort at Gazala was masterful and is accorded due status in this book as his greatest victory, but it is true, as he admitted himself, that his opponent there 'had not completely realised the consequences that follow from the fully motorised conduct of operations and from the open terrain of the desert'. As Liddell Hart has said, the British generals had used former infantry warfare principles in a fast-moving, motorised action.

It was his individualism that made his battles with Bernard Montgomery, and other British commanders, so intriguing; both Monty and Rommel were determined, conscientious and astute, but they were wholly different creatures. While Rommel could become bored by caution and inaction, Montgomery would, if necessary, use both to secure good order on the battlefield and enable his more formal style to dominate. Here it is apposite to remember that the two men had vastly different roles in the 1914–18 War; one learned the value of speed and élan, the other the importance of systematic and traditional organisation.

Blumenson[13] ascribes to Rommel the command characteristics of 'boldness, the use of surprise, a readiness to take risk and an intuitive feel for the battlefield'. He is, of course, right, but it was the first and third of these qualities that were distinctive.

It can perhaps be claimed that his was a character that was galvanised by action, that he was one who quickly came to be driven by achievement and success. Without giving any prior indication that it was to be the case, the young Rommel found his niche on an active battleground, large or small. His first taste of it proved his courage and tenacity to himself and his hunger for more became quickly apparent. Because he hadn't experienced the main battle-fronts of the Great War he had to use the inter-war years to learn the theory of long-range bombardment and the gradual winning of ground by yards at a time and then adapt his natural desire for something more fluid to the potential of the new weaponry. Looking back on the Great War, he became certain that pace around the battlefield was the template for success; the combination of his belief, the mobility of the developing tank warfare and the integration of air support was Blitzkrieg.

We do not know of anything specific that caused him to press for a transfer to the Württembergische Gebirgsbattalion, but his twenty-seven months of service there certainly shaped his combat and command thinking. It has been suggested he never really changed his military philosophy again, that he fought every war as if he were leading a special-purpose unit in the Italian mountains. From that time on, no challenge was too daunting for him, no battle position too hopeless, no colleagues incapable of better performance, and no enemy impervious to challenge.

The mountain unit certainly seemed to awake a latent talent in the young man. Operating much like a special forces battalion would today, using smaller teams with localised tasks and remits, the WG perhaps enabled Rommel to 'cut his command teeth' in small groups where his direct involvement would have an impact, where leadership skill would have a more marked effect. He was quickly at home with the independence it gave him, with mobility a vital part of almost every operation and example-setting leadership and specific goal-setting being encouraged rather than frowned upon. It gave him the courage to be decisive that would not have been afforded to him in the trenches.

His colourful and dramatically successful action at Caporetto gave his reputation, both within the German Army and with the public at home, a massive fillip.

Rommel acclaimed at a rally in Berlin the day after he received his field marshal's baton in September 1942. On his right is Field Marshal Wilhelm Keitel.

By one incident he became a 'name' and assessors and correspondents were immediately predicting great things from this new national hero.

If Rommel's work in Italy in 1917 taught him how to command smaller units, his application of personally managed and driven battlefield tactics on a grander scale were to be quickly tested in 1940. Rommel had not witnessed the primitive tanks' actions of 1918, but that was unnecessary; he simply applied his fighting tenets to his new circumstance.

Auchinleck noted at first-hand Rommel's 'resilience, resourcefulness and mental agility', saying, 'there is much that we can learn from a study of him and his methods',[14] and from his viewpoint Rommel was a general who was solely committed to defeating the enemy. But 'the Auk' and other Allied officers were constant in their opinion that he conducted warfare with an honesty and fairness not so common in many of his compatriots, another way in which he was a very different German general.

So Rommel made few changes to his basic battlefield philosophy throughout his life; he sought to be more active, imaginative and direct than the enemy, using rapid, vigorous moves to wrest the initiative, and personal drive to direct the continuing battle. This practice had been proven in special-forces warfare but, in truth, it was in the scenario of nation versus nation across the fields of another country that the technique of rapid armoured thrust supported by bombers found its perfect operator. For Rommel, the management of a small team on a short, limited operation, or leading a full division in the midst of a larger drive of Army Group proportions was one and the same thing. His constant aim was to drive hard through the enemy's rear and maintain momentum.

Furthermore, there was no change in his style of leadership, for this too remained the same for large or small actions. He liked to be close to the front where he could see his dynamic example and diktats having an effect. If he was occasionally unpredictable it was never a question of whether energy or caution should be used but more that his active mind and the quest for advantage inevitably saw him considering options that would never have occurred to others, here he would perhaps have a change of heart or pursue a fresh initiative rather than risk the most modest delay or inaction.

It is partly because of this unorthodoxy that Rommel never quite achieved the same acclaim and standing in his own country that he did among his enemies. It can be seen in conjunction with the factor that his humble origins meant that he was not always looked upon kindly by the 'vons' – the old guard of Prussian generals who transparently viewed him as something of a renegade, incapable of adhering to the accepted fundamentals of military command. They found it difficult to support the man, whatever results he delivered.

For the advance across Belgium and into France, Rommel was in command of 7th Panzer Division, in Hoth's Panzer Corps, in turn an element of von Rundstedt's Army Group A. His role in the main plan was to protect the right flank of Guderian's Panzer Corps, but this modest task was to become, or to be made, more dramatic as time went by.

The successes were achieved not against inferior or ill-equipped opposition as such – the French had 3,000 tanks. The British Expeditionary Force was not insignificant, but they were fighting an old war, using outdated thinking. Where the Germans had spent the inter-war years considering how the new invention – the tank – could revolutionise warfare, with Guderian and others publishing on the subject, and evolving new tactics for a mobile war of fast-moving armoured firepower, the British and French establishment had not advanced their thinking to the same degree. For them the placement of single or multiples of the machines at strategic locations or moving infantry forward behind a slow phalanx of such vehicles was more likely.

The reason why Rommel is so avidly studied as a military commander is that his techniques were so adaptable that he would have surely been a success in any era on any battlefield. He had fallibilities – occasional hot-headedness when the quest for resolution of a problem overcame the need to consider all possibilities or other alternatives, and a regular intolerance towards supporting officers when they could not assimilate his rapid instructions or deliver his demanded performance. Having said that, he was more often docile and undemonstrative, hiding that inner drive and determination, than he was loud and dictatorial. If you were under the command of Erwin Rommel you knew it! But you were almost certainly grateful for it, especially if you were aware of some of the other options.

Fundamentally, Erwin Rommel merits acclaim as a great military commander for the principal reason of his adaptability. He showed a readiness to move with the technological advances and adapt his strategies to match them, and he was ready to shun accepted traditional military doctrine if he considered it unwise. In his own writings he complains how, for some, a military tenet that had been worked out to the last detail was then regarded for too long as 'the sum of military wisdom', where he would look to amend proven battlefield logic to meet the needs of the day rather than put himself in a strait jacket of conformity.

From the moment when he saw how the tank was likely to develop after its first use, he accepted that it would change the face of warfare. He condemned those who were slow to accept technical progress and insisted that modern commanders should 'be free of all excessive attachment to routine methods and must have an extensive understanding of technical matters'.

Were he alive today one can envisage Rommel being absorbed by debates concerning the non-lethal battlefield, talk of robotics and 'fire-ants', and assessments of how the future warrior might be a 'one-man army' of armour and firepower.

Erwin Rommel was the model of an effective, determined and adaptable military commander.

5
ROMMEL AS A
MANAGER OF MEN

We have seen how ready Erwin Rommel was to set a personal example to his officers and men; no-one can ask more of his or her superior in any walk of life. Although some will classify this as a potential fault or a failure to understand the need to protect the senior man in any situation, most historians believe the trait benefited Rommel rather than caused him problems. He certainly won the respect and admiration of his men from his very first command and the fact that he was prepared to be where he was sending his forces, and confront the same risks he was asking them to take, led to a support that was tangible and beyond measurable value.

German troops outside an improvised cinema in Benghazi.

As a result of his relatively early career success, Rommel was well used to those senior to him seeking his views on matters where he was showing some element of expertise. This inevitably brought some conflict with the older officers, especially those steeped in the formal approaches to war and traditional training. It is to Rommel's credit that he won over so many of the 'old guard', but he would never find favour with them all. This was seen at Caporetto where the Bavarian commanders were not prepared to accept Rommel's cavalier commitment to the unconventional so he had to go over their heads to Major Sprösser who had already seen Rommel's talents at close quarters and was prepared to let him have his head.

A demonstration of Erwin Rommel's concern for his fellow soldier came as early as his time at Stuttgart between the wars when he formed, with two like-minded colleagues, Hartmann and Aldinger, an Old Comrades' Association attached to the Württemberg battalion of which they had all been members. This was not some cosmetic exercise for Rommel, nor a desire to create a new social group, for he was to spend much personal time writing letters and visiting those who had struggled during the post-war years. And it was no quest for personal prestige as evidenced when, at an annual meeting and parade of the Association in 1935, he turned down an invitation by General von Soden, taking the salute, to join him on the dais, preferring to march with his old company.

While Rommel was the complete professional soldier in so many ways, and suitably determined to succeed in battle against any enemy of his nation, he was complimentary about those who fought against him, provided they justified praise. Of the defeated 201 Guards Brigade at Gazala he wrote that they were the 'living embodiment of the positive and negative qualities of the British soldier. An extraordinary bravery and toughness was combined with a rigid inability to move quickly.' And, of course, it was not the fault of the ordinary soldier that he lacked speed of mobility, it was the strategies set in stone from those above, and we have seen elsewhere how scathing the German was of failure of the British officers and planners whose military tactics had not evolved at the same pace as the Germans'.

Despite his independence of spirit, Erwin Rommel relied on his senior officers as much as any general, though there were plenty of occasions when such faith in their soldiering ability was not enough to be persuaded away from a battlefield move he was convinced was right. He writes of the 'bitter loss' suffered when Colonel Westphal was injured at the time of Gazala and was returned to Europe, thus depriving the 'Desert Fox' of a man whose assistance, by the opinion of his commander, was 'of outstanding value, because of his extraordinary knowledge and experience and readiness to take decision.'

Perhaps it needed a particularly skilled individual to gauge when the Swabian was ready to take advice and when he was not. We know from his early days of military training that he was not naturally argumentative in character, and at that time was very eager to listen. He remained one who was sympathetic with his men while expecting exactly the same effort and drive that he showed himself. There is no doubt that he changed his style of command between the time of the race into France and the North African desert, but this was because in the former theatre he was one of several commanders and subject to the nearby decision-making of others. In the desert it was chiefly his show and, not unsurprisingly, he was at his democratic best when things were going well and less likely to show his traditional empathy with his fellow soldiers when being most severely tested.

His man-management was extremely good most of the time. He enjoyed the comradeship of military life, even when it was on a live battlefield for, not being a gregarious character, he appreciated finding himself in a situation where such camaraderie was naturally present.

Rommel with the Italian General Azzi (right).

A German war correspondent is quoted by Desmond Young as describing Rommel having 'a smile and a joke for everyone who seemed to be doing his job

… he had a very warm heart and more charm than any one I have ever known'. And yet if this suggests an overtly easy man to get on with and be managed by, we have seen that this was not entirely so. Because he managed from the front-line – no admiral ever won a sea war from his home base, was a phrase that he lived by – his orders were more often than not given verbally rather than in writing or across the airwaves by a third party, and this could cause confusion and dispute. More than once, his junior officers behind the line would hurry forward with fresh troops, armaments or supplies in response to one instruction only to find that, in the interim, Rommel had changed his mind and now required something completely different.

His generals had to accept the rough with the smooth when working under Rommel, that is for sure. If anything, he showed more consideration for, and perhaps empathy with, the ordinary soldier than he did with his officers. For them he could more readily find a rough tongue and show impatience. It was also an undoubted weakness of his that he could occasionally by-pass a senior officer when giving instructions, though he would surely argue that such instances were only brought about by desperate and urgent circumstances.

Also, some of his officers were of the 'old school' of military hierarchy that Rommel so deplored and this could mean that they were more likely to secure their own battlefield comforts before attending to the orders of the day or the well-being of their men. It was a recipe for some conflict, but seldom became a problem while his command was enjoying success; in days of reversal Rommel could be quick to complain that his officers should be more prepared to 'get their hands dirty' as their commander was always prepared to do. To be fair, almost any of Rommel's generals would be quick to back their leader and confirm his bravery, instinct and intuition and readily put aside those negative issues that they would discuss among themselves. Perhaps the only criticism they would openly voice was that he was almost too frenetic and, in that state, less easy to deal with or talk to.

But this should not be taken to indicate that his men were constantly under a careless and carefree command. Remember, this was a man who was commanding more than 100,000 men on a battlefield neither he or they had trained for, and we are assured that not only were shorthand notes always taken of verbal instructions given, but, normally, these would be followed by a fully written version later. The armies of Rommel were in the hands of a fiercely committed and determined man who was a master of taking the advantage in a battle when none seemed available, of building a reputation among the enemy that left them in awe of him, and of securing a victory by dint of his own military instinct and fighting qualities. It is churlish to seek too much criticism in a man of such charismatic qualities; the vast majority of those who served with him considered it a privilege.

It is worthwhile noting here that such was the performance he secured from the Afrika Korps in North Africa that it was long believed that the force must be one made up of élite, selected professionals. This was not the case, indeed they were recruited in the normal way and, though they were routinely fit and disciplined, they were not well-suited to the North African conditions of incessant heat. (In this respect, the Allies benefited from the use of South African, Indian and Australian forces).

In discussing Rommel as a manager of men we cannot end without making mention of his extreme diligence in the dealing with the prisoners he was so prone to take in vast numbers. Throughout his military career he maintained the very highest of standards in this regard and was never accused of anything other than doing all he could, within the testing times of conflict, for his less successful opponents. Having come so very near to injury and capture on many occasions it was perhaps fitting that he should act in this way, but the fact is that he had such a strong affinity with the fighting man, friend or foe. Whether he could have maintained these standards had SS Divisions been deployed to Africa is open to conjecture. In General Bayerlein's view it would have been a very different war there had the SS been involved, but, as it was, the Afrika Korps seemed to take a pride in dealing correctly with its many prisoners. Only military items were confiscated and all personal possessions returned after a search. Furthermore, when less humane instructions were received from above, they were disregarded.

In his management of his men Rommel applied the same simple, but not simplistic, style that mixed understanding and admiration with tough demands and exhortations. He believed that leadership by example was vital – it had proved to be for him from the moment of his first live action – and that no amount of reading or scientific study could replace the value of natural empathy with subordinates. He was a commander whose only drug was the ecstasy of battle success and he imbued his hard-working men with the same creed. For him the most valuable asset he possessed on the battlefield was not his armour, his ammunition or his supplies, but his men. Their well-being was paramount because it made them better fighters, their enthusiasm was essential for their producing a maximum performance just as a loss of their spirit was akin to the firing mechanism of a weapon becoming rusty.

The sight of the short, confident, effusive leader at the head of his formation was the embodiment of Rommel's man-management philosophy. The surviving veterans of his time in Africa would only ever describe themselves as having been in Rommel's Afrika Korps – the commander's name was always used.

6

ROMMEL AND HIS USE OF WEAPONRY

If his exploits during the Great War were principally undertaken with hand-held and light weapons, and masses of personal drive and resourcefulness, so Erwin Rommel's campaigns in the 1939–45 campaign were founded on the tank. He became a tank man through and through, realising that its effective use brought superiority on the battlefield and that, for all his own wisdom and skill, the better your tanks the greater your chance of victory.

His limited action on the Western Front in the Great War was based around the brilliant and daring use of infantrymen, and some horseback patrols, where rifles and handguns were the principal weapons. Though he himself never claimed great marksmanship skills, Rommel was never slow to fire whatever weapon he had at the time but where he did show greatness was his choice of how and when to employ numbers of armed personnel and any larger guns available to him.

Where even some of the German military hierarchy still looked upon the tank as a 'battering ram' working on behalf of the infantry, Rommel was far more interested in the diversity the new tanks offered. The directed thrusts of Blitzkrieg

A German PzKpfw III Ausf F, armed with the short 50mm gun, which formed the backbone of Rommel's Afrika Korps during the early battles in the desert.

were far more than blunt and lumbering; they could be rapier-like, with sharp central strikes and flanking moves at a pace not available by any other means.

When commanding 7th Panzer Division in 1940, Rommel had at his disposal a panzer regiment, a motorised infantry brigade or two motorised rifle regiments and an artillery regiment, together with battalion-sized reconnaissance, anti-tank, engineer, signals and motor-cycle units. The tanks were:

PzKpfw I	PzKpfw II	PzKpfw 38(t)	PzKpfw IV
2 men, 6 tons	3 men, 10 tons	4 men, 9.4 tons	5 men, 18.8 tons
2 x MG13 and 1 x MG 34 machine-guns	1 x 2cm cannon and 2 x MG34 machine-guns	1 x 3.7cm anti-tank gun and 1 x MG34 machine-gun	1 x 7.5cm gun and 1 x MG34 machine-gun
Max. speed 40kph Range 140km	Max. speed 55kph Range 200km	Max. speed 40kph Range 250km	Max. speed 40kph Range 200km

The much valued artillery support consisted of three 4-gun batteries of FH18 10.5cm field howitzers in each of its two battalions. The anti-tank teams used 37mm guns and anti-aircraft units worked with truck mounted/towed FlaK guns of 20mm or 80mm. By the time of his arrival in the Desert, Rommel's 5th Light Division had a strength of 155 tanks of which the most numerous were PzKpfw IIs of which he had 45 and PzKpfw IIIs of which he held 61. The 15th Panzer Division had 146 tanks of which again the most numerous were the IIs and IIIs.

Two disabled German PzKpfw IV Ausf Es being inspected by Allied personnel.

It was not simply the principles of tank warfare that Rommel had studied so deeply. He was, by common consent of those he commanded, as knowledgeable about the workings of a tank, or anti-aircraft gun, as many of the mechanics who worked on them or the ranking soldiers who fought in them; if Erwin Rommel told his men a tank could travel a specific route in a particular time, or fire at a quoted range or speed, it was because he knew it could. He would often position himself in front-line vehicles under fire to demonstrate to his men his confidence in their durability. And, just as he would help his engineers build a temporary bridge across a river under attack, he would also guide and assist in tank and gun maintenance during the heat of battle. In all this the Desert Fox was something of a one-off for few generals in the forces of either combatant group had his technical knowledge, even fewer kept such expertise up-to-date and fewer again would dirty their hands to help their lowly gunner crews.

To suggest that Rommel used the weapons at his disposal as a Grand Master might move his chess pieces around a board is not without some accuracy, though it does suggest a certain regimentation and a distancing from his men, and we know that was not the German's way. He certainly applied the depth of thought to the positions on the battlefield as a chess player might his board, but he was more akin to the player-manager who might be employed to coach a sports team but is also expected to play in matches himself. He would not, however, then sit back and watch the outcome but re-position his assets, manage the change from defence to attack and call for particular moves that could bring about the desired result.

The Allied assessment of Rommel's use of his men and machines often reached the point of undiluted admiration. In a report by 7th Armoured Division at the end of 1941 it was observed that the co-ordination of anti-tank guns, field artillery, infantry and tanks produced 'all-arms teams' of great effect, and that every movement of vehicles was escorted by an outer screen of tanks and an inner screen of anti-tank guns, but went on to say that their columns would undertake long night marches to limit their vulnerability to attack – Rommel's much-used additional 'weapons' in the desert were darkness and dust/sand storms – and that their method of withdrawal could not easily cope with concerted pursuit against their flanks.

It was not Rommel's faulty use of his weaponry that led to the German defeat in North Africa. After enjoying early dominance of his German tanks over those available to the British, and making do as best he could with the poorer quality Italian machines he inherited, it was the arrival on the scene of quantities of the American vehicles that contributed to defeat in a major way. The Tiger tanks, much vaunted by Hitler in meetings with Rommel, were never to make the impact they might have done had Germany's priorities included the North African theatre.

At the time of the decisive Alamein battle it can be seen just how bereft of tanks and guns Rommel was. While Montgomery could call on 170 Grant and 252 Sherman tanks supplied by the US under the Lend-Lease Agreement, as well as a further 600 assorted machines, Rommel could barely muster 200 of German origin. His own list suggested that he required during September and October, though knew he wouldn't get them, 11,200 men, 3,200 vehicles including modern tanks, 70 field guns and 65,000 tons of supplies. As it was, his head count would be barely into six figures of which fewer than half were German.

There is no doubt that Erwin Rommel was one of Germany's finest tank masters. His intimate knowledge of tank and gun mechanics and performance meant that his disposition of his armour resources was more efficient and astute than most of his fellow commanders. His intuition on the battlefield, interwoven with his technical abilities, made light of the weaponry imbalance time after time, his opponents often believing they were facing greater firepower than was the case. His certainty when directing artillery fire was legendary and, of course, he quickly showed in his tank work how much better he had learned to use the modern machines than his Allied opponents.

Erwin Rommel was a modern infantryman who fully used and understood the latest armour and artillery and found that the concept of employing it in fast-moving, multi-disciplinary tactics entirely matched his quick-witted and energetic approach to the battlefield.

A German 88mm gun destroyed by British artillery. Designed as an AA gun, it proved to be a powerful anti-tank gun and played a crucial role in Rommel's desert campaign.

7

ROMMEL AND
HIS OPPONENTS

General Montgomery

Bernard Montgomery was almost the direct opposite of Erwin Rommel. Both were small men and each had seen action in the Great War, albeit of very different type, but there were few other similarities apart from the obvious ones of determination, resilience and the ability to plan battlefield action. While Rommel's reputation has, if anything, grown over recent years, Montgomery's has reduced to some degree. Blumenson[15] considers Monty 'competent, adequate (but) he was not great (and) vastly over-rated, the most over-rated general of World War Two'.

Nicknamed 'Monkey' at St Paul's School – housed in buildings that were later to be used for the planning of the Normandy Invasion – his transfer to Sandhurst brought a cadet life that was none too distinguished, and was certainly less so than some of those he would end up commanding. Ranked only 36th at the time of his passing out, he was unable to obtain the place in an Indian Regiment that he sought and had to opt for the Royal Warwickshire Regiment with whom he was to serve in the British Expeditionary Force in 1914. He was awarded the DSO when his platoon captured the village of Meteren by means of a bayonet charge.

His despair at some of the tragedies of the 1914–18 conflict developed his determination to work in a well-planned and orderly way and it was this track record that would come to earn the respect and trust of his troops. He slowly learned how to work with his fellow man, for it had not come easy to him in his youth, and succeeding superiors felt required to regularly issue warnings about the need to avoid the high-handedness he was prone to show.

It was seen in his taking over from Auchinleck that he was neither an observer of certain etiquettes that were normally observed on such occasions, nor slow to relish the opportunity to take control. He was critical of sub-standard performance in all aspects of military life, as was Rommel, and did not hesitate to identify examples when he found them, again like the German. If he set himself against a junior officer that man was usually condemned for ever; Rommel was known to offer second chances on occasions. And Montgomery was seen at his intolerant worst when he came to work with the Americans where, frankly, there was never any hope of more than grudging acceptance of the need to work together; Rommel suffered the Italians in a similar way, especially when he first arrived in Africa.

But they were vastly different men on and off the battlefield. Where Rommel directed his men from close quarters, Montgomery favoured the occasional, often sudden, visit to the front-line. Rommel spoke with a soldier's energy and generated the support of his men by his natural empathy with their work; Monty had a more formal approach and used large-scale gatherings to preach assurance and confidence. Both men broke free of these patterns from time to time but this highlights their different styles.

These two men had both studied their history, each being well acquainted with Napoleon, and Montgomery with the Colonial wars, Rommel with the Franco-Prussian War. Each had his historical heroes, but both were their own men, making their own decisions and unlikely to be unduly swayed by past military masters.

When Montgomery arrived in North Africa he found his men were in awe of the enemy, or more particularly of its commander. This, on top of the British

Not until Montgomery arrived in the desert, and had received adequate reinforcements of men and equipment, did the Allies eject Rommel from Egypt and Cyrenaica.

forces being demoralised and under-equipped, meant that he faced a forbidding challenge. Within a month of his arrival, however, he brought his diligent planning and newly arrived men and equipment to bear at Alam Halfa where he arrested Rommel's advance towards Cairo. Two months later, he was able to go on to the counter-attack at El Alamein and bring Britain's first success of the war.

With Rommel now suffering from a real lack of support from Berlin, the British commander was able to force the issue and saw his opponent extracted from North Africa before he could undertake any final defence of the territory he had so dominated. Montgomery, with his two extra British divisions and new

Field Marshal Sir Harold Alexander (left) and Lieutenant-General Bernard Montgomery.

quantities of advanced tanks and guns, became a national hero, though it is still debated whether or not his predecessors could have secured the victory earlier, given this extra resource.

The two would never again confront each other at close quarters, though Rommel was dashing around Normandy in a vain attempt to stem the Allied breakout when he was seriously injured and prevented from further active participation in the war. As Rommel was most at home in the desert where his tactical acumen and personal drive matched the responsibility given to him, so Montgomery's plain but determined strategies saw him attain international respect for securing the first land victory against Germany and thus deflate the German's ever-growing reputation of invincibility.

Claude Auchinleck (left) and Archibald Wavell studying a map. Both men had considerable qualities, but neither of them was able to defeat Rommel decisively.

General Auchinleck

As Rommel's star has generally risen in the 57 years since his death, Auchinleck's has, of late, suffered. The 'soldier's soldier', as 'the Auk' was often called, has had his reputation dented by historians and by his contemporaries such as Alanbrooke, whose diaries[16] are none too kind, and Churchill who, of course, had to sack him.

When Auchinleck replaced Wavell he was slow to set out the means by which he would achieve plans and objectives and continued to show a weakness in the very type of clear strategic thought and planning that was needed. His appointment of General Alan Cunningham, who had no experience of tanks, to command the Eighth Army is difficult to understand given that General Wilson was available and a more logical choice; within weeks he was forced to replace Cunningham with Major-General Ritchie.

Almost in spite of Auchinleck's prevarication and indecision, Rommel lost out in Operation 'Crusader' and had to abandon Bardia and Halfaya and, after Tobruk was relieved and Benghazi recaptured, had been forced to sacrifice his gains of a year before. But Rommel still prized Tobruk and made more moves for it in early 1942, and in doing so brought more confusion to Auchinleck who appeared unable to effect a strategy for its retention in among the wider schemes for North Africa. Rommel's single-mindedness contrasted acutely with Auchinleck's indecision, and Rommel was in control at his front-line while his British counterpart was well back behind his lines issuing instructions to the still-learning Ritchie.

Tobruk was as dominant in Auchinleck's desert work as it was in Rommel's. He spoke of the defenders of the port 'behaving not as a hardly pressed garrison but as a spirited force ready at any moment to launch an attack, they contained an enemy force twice their strength'. Claude Auchinleck suffered, like Wavell, from insufficient men and *matériel* to complete the task he was given, but, though he earned respect from his men for his reluctance to commit too much too often, his caution that at times seemed to warrant the description of lethargy meant that the patience of the politicians finally ran out.

General Wavell

This intelligent man might have been classed as a similar personality to Rommel during the years of peace for he was, like the German, quiet, undemonstrative and studious. The similarities ended, however, when it came to war for Archibald Percival Wavell remained unspectacular and rather formal when he needed to be tough, decisive and determined. This caused the politicians, especially Churchill, to be suspicious of his effectiveness as a battlefield decision-maker.

But Rommel was complimentary, especially with regard to Wavell's action against the Italians which he described as a model of 'bold planning and daring execution with small resources'. He was right, of course, for that was Wavell's finest moment even though it was against less demanding opposition than he would encounter once the German arrived on the scene. It was to be the Allies' only significant success until Alamein.

Wavell's situation in North Africa was weakened by the need to send many of his troops on the ill-advised expedition to Greece, and the fact that this coincided with Rommel's arrival in the desert meant that he was always facing his greatest trial with far too few resources. His offensive from Egypt into Libya in

September 1940 had mauled the Italian Army, but the German and his troops were an entirely different prospect, and would have been even if Wavell had received the replacement forces he had needed to redress the balance. What we shall never know is whether a more sympathetic regime in London, or more time, men and *matériel*, would have enabled this calm administrator to become a more permanently successful Commander-in-Chief.

After further problems in the summer of 1941, Churchill transferred Wavell to the Far East, having become convinced, perhaps rightly, that for all his planning and diligence, he was not a natural man of war.

Wavell was a more competent commander than many give him credit for, but he was a natural planner and organiser rather than a soldier.

General Ritchie

Neil Ritchie had little command experience when he was thrown into the furnace of the North African campaign as replacement for Alan Cunningham as Commander of Eighth Army. He suffered various reversals before Auchinleck,

Neil Ritchie was not well qualified for the role given to him at the time of Rommel's Gazala success. His dispositions were ill-chosen and his response to enemy moves slow and disjointed.

for whom Ritchie had been acting as Assistant Chief of Staff in Cairo, had to take back control himself. Ritchie was found to be utterly swamped by Rommel's manoeuvres at Gazala, proving incapable of either setting out his formations with good sense and logic or reacting effectively to the enterprising initiatives of the German.

General O'Connor

Richard O'Connor had been commanding 7th Armoured Division in Palestine and was Governor of Jerusalem when war broke out. In 1940 he was sent with his men to Egypt where he became commander of the Western Desert Force under Wavell, who acted as something of a sponsor to the younger man. These two had great success against the Italians in December 1940 but found Rommel an altogether tougher opponent. O'Connor was ambushed and captured by the Germans at the outset of Rommel's first invasion of Cyrenaica and not released until 1943. But for this incarceration, he would have surely played a greater part in the Allied efforts against Rommel.

Churchill visits Egypt. On the left is Sir Harold Alexander. Lieutenant-General Montgomery is to the right of Churchill. On the far right is Sir Alan Brooke.

ROMMEL: THE HISTORICAL PERSPECTIVE

As we have mentioned, Erwin Rommel wrote as well he fought; his accounts of his career are characteristically vivid and well-proven as accurate and authoritative. Remarkably he chose not to unduly embellish his considerable achievements – would that this was the case with all memoirs – but then perhaps he knew that the truth was sufficient to mark his as a worthy military career.

Certainly he was aware, if unlikely to have made too much of it, that his reputation influenced his opponents to an unhealthy degree. He owned a translation of Auchinleck's letter to 'All Commanders and Chiefs of Staff' in which the British Commander-in-Chief claimed: 'There exists a real danger that our friend Rommel is becoming a kind of magician or bogeyman to our troops, who are talking far too much about him. He is by no means a superman, though he is undoubtedly very energetic and able … I wish you to dispel by all possible means the idea that Rommel represents something more than an ordinary German general.'

It was clearly correct for Auchinleck to issue such a directive though even he knew he was up against rather more than 'an ordinary general'. Indeed it was not just within the ranks of the German Army that Rommel was unique; few British commanders had such a desire to work in the front-line with their men, preferring the traditional code that expected them to direct the action from well behind the lines, relying on reports and messages from others. Even the less formal Americans followed a similar practice, save perhaps Patton and a handful of others.

Indeed, Rommel's unique battlefield management style was roundly condemned by many of his contemporaries. Churchill refers back to his performance in junior education as unspectacular, that 'mentally he was not remarkable' and, with such comment, perhaps suggests his methods of generalship were a counter for his lack of deep intellect. It is possible to concede that his manic attitude in battle was something of a compensation for the lack of theoretical depth in his strategic thinking that might be required to stand back from the front-line and plan and monitor as a general would normally do.

Lieutenant-General Brian Horrocks notes, with others, that a great many officers resented his interference with their commands and that they often could not find him at crucial times of a battle when his location should have been known to all who might need his direction. He, like several military men, criticises the German's involvement in battle action and claims that it caused him to fail to appreciate the larger picture. But the same writer, like so many other army professionals and historians, bows to Rommel's strengths according him the epithet of the 'best armoured corps commander produced by either side. Utterly fearless, full of drive and initiative, always up at the front where the battle was the fiercest. If his opponent made a mistake, Rommel was on it like a flash.'

Opposite page: A typical Churchillian gesture during a visit to the Allied forces in North Africa.

General Harold Alexander who, more than most, knew how hard the Allied forces had been pressed by the man from Heidenheim, paid a similar compliment when he said that 'there is no question that the Field Marshal was a most able battle commander'. He was, like Auchinleck, dismissive of the almost mythical status given to the Desert Fox by even his own men, saying that although Rommel was undoubtedly 'a wizard on the battlefield ... it was hardly necessary to attribute to him preternatural gifts in order to explain his success'.

History has tended to accept that Erwin Rommel was a one-off, having been fed this assessment by war correspondents and historians as well as colleagues and opponents. That some cannot allow this to be an entirely complimentary term is disappointing and surely stems from the impact he had during his own career, both within his own country and beyond. Not since Napoleon had an enemy so stirred the British nation, from its simplest foot soldiers to its politicians and rulers; within Germany, its formal military traditionalists were undoubtedly taken aback by some of Rommel's unorthodox ways, the reputation he seemed to gain so easily, and, at the last, the choice he made to end his own life.

Rommel outside Tobruk alongside an Italian M13/40 tank.

We have seen that Rommel did not even enjoy unblemished praise for his dramatic exploits in the Great War, and we can see how, again, his somewhat cavalier approach to war and command there left an uncomfortable taste in the mouths of formal colleagues and superiors who were not capable of such resourcefulness so found it difficult to give credit for it when it was displayed. In the 1939–45 conflict he was not alone in the higher military ranks in failing to show the desired unswerving commitment to the Nazi cause, but, as evidenced in others such as Guderian and von Rundstedt, some generals were just too valuable for Hitler to leave under-utilised by the Reich war machine. What Rommel was ambitious for was the national standing; this is what drove him, and this was sufficient to keep him focused. Those campaigning more vigorously against the Hitler regime and his war policies became despondent by the limits Rommel placed on his endorsement of their schemes and perhaps were thus stimulated into claiming, under interrogation, a greater involvement for him and thus bringing about his suicide.

That he had such impact and success in both World Wars certainly places Rommel in another unique band for few recorded his level of achievement in both conflicts, and none did so as a dashing field officer on both occasions. It was not by accident that during the 1939–45 War he rose from Lieutenant-Colonel to Field Marshal in four years; it was because his achievement against the odds made such promotions inevitable.

Manfred Rommel, quoted by Ronald Lewin, said that the one certainty to which his father adhered in planning was that the unexpected would certainly happen tomorrow, and that there was a large allowance for contingency in his father's thinking. And this perhaps discloses the reason for adverse comments from some contemporaries and more recent assessors.[17] As Churchill noted, Rommel would say, in answer to the claim that he acted impetuously and often against orders, that it was always his policy to 'issue orders in accordance with what the situation demanded'. It is not always easy for the top man to admit that he might have to change his plans on a whim, on an unforeseen happenstance, preferring to insist that he has planned for every possibility. This is a claim of fools who lessen their renown by such brazen self-importance and that was not a character failing Rommel suffered from. If he was not the brightest of intellects he knew how best to apply the talents he did have and one suspects Churchill's high regard for the man stems from his seeing similarities between the two and regarding the German's adaptability and affinity with his men as attributes he himself had.

When Mussolini sought German assistance in Africa, Adolf Hitler decided to send Erwin Rommel. This must have been seen as a gamble and may well have been done to get this spiky individual out from under the feet of the coterie of dour sycophants and military traditionalists that surrounded the Führer. One imagines that the reservations expressed at the appointment were countered by Hitler's assuring doubters that a careful eye would be kept on the commander by the leader's own trusted confidants being placed in theatre with him and the regular recall for thorough reports and briefing. Even so, a modern business supremo would be reluctant to appoint such a maverick to his furthest branch office.

John Keegan and many more have stated that Rommel was 'perfectly attuned' for the Blitzkrieg strategy. In using it so astutely the German was simply progressing his attitude to fighting in the Great War, for there he moved stealthily, speedily, and struck with lethal opportunism and accuracy. When land armour and aircraft were the weapons available to him he simply employed them with similar cunning, using the element of surprise and pace with the same dexterity as he had done those years before.

Ironically, for one so content to operate 'on the hoof', Rommel was often critical of the Allies for failing to spend enough time on training and was of the opinion that many of his triumphs and advantages came from British errors aggravated by lack of attention to detail. He simply felt that the British were hampered by old-fashioned views and practices and in this he is supported by Auchinleck who complained that the British had not used the inter-war years for thinking and planning, whereas the Germans had done so. Thus, Rommel was entirely in tune with the new ways of making war, and so were his staff officers, while the British were still struggling to understand what mobile warfare really was and how it was best used. He was always checking to ensure that men in his charge knew their weapons both technically and logistically and, wherever possible, gave them enough time for familiarisation training.

The Desert War saw pure tank versus tank combat in unique terrain that the designers of the weapons may not have originally planned for. The circumstances called for a commander who was adaptable and practical, not one who was likely to spend time pushing theoretical thought around a planning table and questioning how the tank used through the Ardennes and into France and now likely to be seen on the vast landscapes of Eastern Europe, could be deployed in the wide open spaces of North Africa. What the situation called for was a practical man who understood how flexible the battle tank could be in the right hands.

Rommel had seen in Belgium and France that infantry could only combat the tank from well-prepared positions and quickly saw that the desert would seldom provide protection of any sort. Thus, the warfare would often be genuine tank versus tank action, with the quality and number of vehicles being the principal advantage and the intuition of the commander coming into play.

The German was the perfect man to revise rapidly his strategy and gain the upper hand against less flexible opponents. He realised, for a start, that 'in Libya and Egypt there arose certain laws, fundamentally different from those in other theatres'. He also experienced in Africa the anguish of having inferior air forces, and saw how the tank could lose its effectiveness in open ground if constantly harassed from overhead. He was seldom able to employ the full Blitzkrieg tactics for this very reason; where in France the Luftwaffe ably supported the tank divisions and the infantry, in the desert Rommel hardly ever had the chance to hustle his opponents by land *and* air, which makes his achievements all the more remarkable.

At times in North Africa Rommel found 'British air superiority threw to the winds all our operational and tactical rules because they no longer applied … there was no answer to the problem of dealing with the enemy air superiority'. With full justification he quoted Allied air strength as being the deciding factor in the region for it eroded the advantage of the Desert Fox's own brilliance on the battlefield, made his every move risk laden and vulnerable, and damaged a constantly weak supply situation.

It is difficult to imagine Rommel fighting in any other way than he did in North Africa, but, to large measure, it was forced upon him. He appeared to envy Montgomery's opportunity to pause and plan, whereas he seldom had had the chance to do so to the degree he would have wished. With a permanently dire supply situation he was often forced to 'go with what he had' and, in this, he was a master. For John Strawson, Rommel was 'a brave and brilliant tactical commander in fluid, mobile battles … His flair for sensing where and when the enemy was weak and uncertain, his instinctive concentration and personal grip at the front during critical times, his implacable drive, his chivalry, above all his opportunism – these are the things for which the Desert Fox will be remembered.[18]

When assessing Rommel's performance there, one has to take into account the dramatic changes that his enemies were undergoing, and most historians, as well as veterans of the events, have attended to this. When he arrived in the region the German was given minimal resources plus an allied force of Italians that had just been humbled by the British. His mixed forces could hardly perform worse than the Italians had done on their own and, to accentuate matters, his opponents were then decimated by the removal of a large number of all ranks to the Greek campaign. For the first few months it was easy for Rommel, even with his modest resources of men and *matériel* to make an impact. By the end of the North African war, however, he was fighting the great organiser and motivator, Alexander, and the diligent planner and executioner, Montgomery, and doing so with a force not so much stronger than he had had at the start and one that had suffered constant shortages. One commentator has said that all Rommel ever needed to win the war in North Africa was a regular supply of ironmongery; if he had had that in the first year of his work there he might well have been the victor in that theatre.

Rommel was not prepared for the pace and extent of the Allied reinforcement before Alamein, but retrospectively noted that it was clear that those administering his opponents had come to the conclusion that decisive action was vital, and the required resources must be provided. It was determination he had never seen from German High Command and that, and the ongoing under-performance of his Italian allies, was a major contribution to the inevitably of defeat.

After he left North Africa Rommel was to say that he had no arguments with Italian soldiers, particularly those he was able to influence by his direct man-

An Allied truck comes under shellfire as it edges through a minefield. Such open country made for easy targeting.

agement, and was mostly content with the junior officers and generals. It was the state system, the political hierarchy and the poor equipment that caused his despair and weakened the spine of the men in the ranks.

Erwin Rommel continued to serve his country despite his disgust with the High Command's assessment of the defeat at El Alamein. He could not understand how he and his soldiers could be held entirely responsible rather than the shortage of supplies, lack of air support or the implausible directives that had

pressed for a 'last stand'. In his writings he complains of having been adjudged a defeatist, and assumes such criticism stemmed from the many quarrels and disputes brought about by his constant demands for more support and supplies. As a true battlefield commander he never enjoyed the best of relationships with desk-bound paper-pushers who were not experiencing 'live war'.

Because the commanders of the Allied forces did not change the basic principles by which they fought against him throughout the Desert War, Rommel was right to feel he could manufacture a victory from seemingly poor positions. With their standard patterns and policies, they were predictable and could be 'managed' with less than ideal resources, but, in the end, the big battle at El Alamein was one of *matériel* rather than will and determination.

At this vital battle, Rommel claimed the opposition did not mount an 'operation' as he understood it but simply set up a situation where their artillery and air force would be decisive. He was further perplexed by the reluctance of Montgomery to pursue the Axis retreat and, before that, his refusal to commit all his tanks in the cause of the swift victory it would have surely brought. He seemed to believe that, in view of the men and equipment he lost because of his reservation, Montgomery should have earned more criticism than praise for what was seen as his greatest victory.

Michael Howard and others are of the view that the Allied success in North Africa dramatically altered the British and American governments' attitude for the rest of the European war, and certainly accelerated the oft-debated landings in Italy. When Rommel flew home from North Africa he must have felt that he had done all he could, retaining his firm belief in his own actions but now fearful for the future of his country. Instead of Germany's forces sweeping around the Mediterranean to meet up with other Third Reich units, it would be Allied armies landing in Sicily, crossing to Italy and, in time, landing in northern and southern France.

It seems such a strange appointment now – Erwin Rommel, the great mobile warrior, put in charge of static defences. Hitler had sought to use him in Italy, but, by then, the star of Albert Kesselring was shining somewhat brighter and, despite continuing admiration for the man, the Führer eventually decided to give the Swabian the task of shoring up the 'Atlantic Wall'.

It is fitting, but somewhat ironic, that it was Rommel and not the diehard traditionalist, von Rundstedt, who called the right location for the Allied landing when it came. The Desert veteran was bringing his recent extensive battlefield experience to the debate while the veteran Prussian was still employing historical theory; the first a tactical approach, the latter one of strategic bias. It is now seen that, had Rommel had his way, the Normandy landings could have been very much more difficult to achieve than they were. The fact that the man of the desert had moved so swiftly into his new role, *and assessed what the right tactics would have been*, is testament to his flexibility and in-bred ability to evaluate a battle situation.

It was a sad consequence of circumstances that Archibald Wavell was removed from the North African theatre before he had the chance to get to grips with the fighting phenomenon that was Erwin Rommel. Although a vastly different character from the German, Wavell *was* similar in military attitude and concepts to Montgomery and it might have been an interesting contest had it come about. Both men had similar views about the role of the general in respect of his soldiers; they both held the opinion that the general should be of a character that the men would follow, from whom they could draw courage and enthusiasm, and who was more concerned with the safety of the men and belief in what they could achieve than calculating how many of them he might lose. This does not mean that Rommel was profligate with the lives of his men, but that, just the opposite, he would lead them to action if he felt he and they had a chance of victory rather than spend so long assessing the risks that the chance of success was lost and the danger to the men's lives even worse. He was often heard to remark that his nation would 'need these men after the war as well as during it' and this is what directed his thinking.

The 'Rommel' Phenomenon

There have been many military leaders who have been far more concerned about their own reputation than Rommel. If Napoleon ensured his own versions of his exploits were published before those that might not be so complimentary, and today's military leaders have to have an ability to communicate to the world media, Erwin Rommel was completely undemonstrative when it came to talking and writing of his own exploits. He preferred to write in private to his wife in order to release from his mind his considerations of the troubles of the day and his accounts were invariably modest in tone, be they of achievement or setback.

So it was not by his own propagation that the very word 'Rommel' came to instil such fear in his enemies and hero-worship in his own land. It can be argued that others of his generation were greater innovators, even better battlefield strategists; those who claim Guderian was a far greater military genius have a case because he certainly had a greater mastery of the theories. But his enemies did not make mention of Heinz Guderian in their political debating chamber, nor invent so eye-catching a nickname as 'the Desert Fox'. It was Churchill's speech, Auchinleck's note to his commanders and chiefs of staff, and the manner in which such observations gathered substance and meaning, that created the legend.

Adolf Hitler realised the significance of the phenomenon and the reasons for its creation, saying that 'the mere name [of Rommel] suddenly begins to acquire the value of several divisions.' Such is a measure, if not the whole measure, of greatness for we often see nowadays that the media believes that if one player in a sports team is playing in a particular match, its result is almost a foregone conclusion. Once a reputation is formed, and the modern media seems to be solely driven by fame and repute, it really does create a power of its own and exerts an influence beyond reality. If a star actor is unable to appear in a film or play the director or audience might feel the performance is damaged, or if he does appear the result will certainly be a positive one, though this is seldom the case. It could certainly be argued that if Germany's star performer had been lost from the North African contest, or had had to be withdrawn for any reason, his 'cast's' performance would have been very different, and surely less successful.

As this volume has demonstrated, Rommel earned his reputation by the bravura nature of his fighting. From Caporetto to Normandy he showed great resolve, imagination and resilience and for this his own men admired him and his enemy feared him. The first question the simple Allied infantryman would often ask as he prepared for action was 'is Rommel around?' and the distant cloud of dust that heralded a German tank advance was often announced as 'here comes Rommel'. Defeats and reversals suffered at his hands almost came to be accepted because it was he who had headed the offensive and, likewise, any element of success against enemy forces when it was known the Desert Fox had been on the field was treated with great celebration.

The phenomenon was created from local renown and grew through national and international public acknowledgement; if a tank crew in the Desert tell each other 'this Rommel is a good general' it spreads no farther than the regiment, but if Winston Churchill proclaims that the man is a 'very daring and skilful opponent … and a great general' the world takes notice.

The fact of hero worship brings both advantage and disadvantage and just as today we seem to create our heroes only to knock them from the pedestals on which they have been placed, in the Second World War, the greater the Rommel legend became the more he had to do to protect it. The slightest error was watched for, especially by the hawk-eyed enemies he had in German High Command but also by the enemy. Every unorthodox move, every outlandish gamble, was studied and greeted with howls of derision, muted admiration or wholesale celebration depending on its result.

For all the admiration, Rommel's style of instinctive, off-the-cuff command meant the battle area could be confused, with his immediate deputies often not knowing where he was or what personal initiative he was currently pursuing, without keeping them informed. It is not something a von Rundstedt, a Bradley, an Allenby or a Montgomery would have considered doing for these were men who believed a war zone should be as orderly as it could be. But for Rommel good order took time he could ill afford and was, in any case, what the enemy was most confident with. Rommel delighted in surprising the enemy with the unorthodox and, most of the time, his men were content with it too.

The deepest doubts that continue to surround the reputation of Erwin Rommel concern the fact that he never held command of the great formations that were seen, in particular, on the Eastern Front. In the relatively small confines of North Africa and the comparatively small numbers of men he had to manage and direct, Rommel cannot be said to have had the most daunting

command task the war provided. Many believe that he would have struggled to apply his campaign methods with greater numbers of men in a broader battle-zone; others say we must assess him only on what he did, not what historians believe he would or would not have done in different circumstances. What the generals of the great Panzer divisions had to do was plan, for they couldn't fight in the *ad hoc* fashion of Rommel, could not control so large a force so single-handedly, and if Rommel had been sent to the Russian Front he would have had to adapt. But, having said that, Rommel himself spoke of North Africa as the theatre of operations where the war took on its most modern shape, causing him to learn new lessons, employ the principles of Blitzkrieg in a scenario that had not been considered when it was devised, and generally show a flexibility some of his more formal and traditional colleagues would have struggled to demonstrate.

Those who have most accurately judged Rommel have assessed actualities, not imagined what might have been, and it is those whose opinions this writer has appreciated most. If they assert that he was not the greatest strategist or the most conscientious planner, but accept that he was one of the finest cavalry commanders in the first war of the tank, and rates alongside the great military action men of the 20th century, they share our view.

Field Marshal Erwin Rommel with his wife, Lucia, and son, Manfred.

THE INGLORIOUS END

Erwin Rommel has confused historians because he was a conundrum. No-one saw his greatness coming, at least not those who knew him in his youth. It is somewhat frustrating to find so few indicators that the military cadet – remember his father persuaded him to take a military career, it was not something he craved or considered himself 'made for' – was destined for greatness. Something happened to the young Rommel when he first tasted military life, and then something amazing occurred when he faced his first battle.

Even then, the devilment that marked his personal drive and command skills on the battlefield appear to have lain contentedly dormant throughout the inter-war years with no overt allegiance to the burgeoning Nazi cause, only a desire to serve his nation and its armed forces. We can even say that he did not strive for a role in Hitler's early military moves, though perhaps his close vicinity to the Führer in those days was power enough.

Had Hitler not read Rommel's book, or not enjoyed it and marked its author as someone worth cultivating, would the future 'Fox' have reached the high command posts he did? One has to believe that he would have, though it might have taken him longer; he certainly benefited from his leader's sponsorship and the way it opened routes that the military hierarchy might have chosen to have kept closed. He might not have been able to show his skills so clearly in the Blitzkrieg years and thus might not have been considered 'ready' for the desert without the benefit of the Führer's 'fast track'. But most successful careers have instances of good fortune and the ability to maximise it. In Rommel's case he edged his leader into acknowledging that he was wasting the talents of a fine soldier by keeping him in command of his personal bodyguard, though it was not typical of the Führer to ask anyone what job they would like. Hitler thought to ask, Rommel had the courage to answer. It was good fortune, well used.

When the time came that overwhelming odds were ranged against him Rommel had to concede and, at the end in Europe, he could not prevent the enemy – one that was out-numbering him in men and with amounts of equipment and air- and sea-power support he could only dream of – from advancing on his homeland. He deserved better than to be ruined by the testimony of bitter men, but the die was cast at a time when the Führer was demented with fears and doubts about so many of his senior men. Even he, in saner times, might have counter-balanced the scales of his dictatorial justice with his own knowledge of Rommel's dedication to the cause; he could and should have prevented so fine a career from coming to such a wretched, pitiful end.

The Desert Fox ended his life in such horrible circumstances that one feels angered all these years on. A sophisticated and advanced nation regrets the evil of wars and the deaths they cause, and honours those of all sides that fought bravely. No one who faced Erwin Rommel across the field of battle would have wished such a sorry end and those he fought with were entitled to feel disenchanted and embittered when the truth became known.

Rommel had returned from Africa a dismayed and dispirited man for not only had Hitler denied him the means of getting a better result there but the Führer's close band of subservients who, Rommel would have reminded himself regularly, had not seen action for many a year if at all – had contributed to the under-resourcing of their colleague in far off North Africa and looked disdainfully upon his suspect allegiance to the Nazi cause. Whatever his views of Hitler prior to his last months in Africa, he now knew that his leader was a blinkered, bigoted and manic egotist who was beyond the point where good reason and sound argument counted for anything.

Back in Europe and thus closer to national military and security policy, he became aware of what was being done in Germany and some other parts of Europe in the cause of Nazism, and understood entirely that this was not what he had served his country for. Rommel was a gentleman warrior; cruelty, extermination, slave labour and gross intolerance of the contrary view was not part of his creed. Bravely, perhaps naively, he confronted Hitler with his opinion that such wretchedness earned only defeat and that he risked losing an entire generation of young men who should mould the future of his country. Seeing the intransigence in his leader, Rommel at least then knew where the fault and responsibility lay and it stirred him to deep thought about how to arrest such terrible decline.

That he accepted a posting to Army Group B in Italy, briefly, and then France, shows that Rommel was still content to be fighting for his nation at that time. We know that close friends and new acquaintances then began exerting greater pressure on him to make his growing disillusionment official and join the ranks of those organising opposition to Hitler, and we know he declined overt involvement, refusing point-blank to become a figurehead of the group. He apparently approached his new appointment of assessing coastal defences with typical vigour, but, inevitably, his gloomy view of current national policy continued to draw him towards those of like mind, to those who were more active in their plotting to force a change of leadership, let alone national strategy. For these people the recruitment of a national, even international, star would hugely benefit their cause, but it seemed they would have to content themselves with his adding his voice to the calls for making peace with the Western Allies.

Dr Karl Strölin had served with Rommel in 1918, and had been Mayor of Stuttgart since 1933. He was a leading player in the growing band of conspirators against Hitler and was the go-between used by them to get to Rommel. Strölin had Frau Rommel show her husband a paper he had written and submitted to the government urging that Nazi persecution be ended, that civil rights be restored and justice returned to the professionals. This note succinctly expressed Rommel's fears for his country and he agreed to meet Strölin. During a long meeting, Rommel was persuaded to seek another meeting with the Führer during which he would effectively take on the role of leader of the disenchanted and urge a change of course – but this is all Rommel undertook to do. Despite his urgings, Strölin could not convince the Field Marshal that he was the only one with the necessary charisma and following to lead an open challenge to the status quo.

During 1944 Rommel was living an astonishing double life. He was charged by Hitler with countering the approaching Allied invasion and yet, at the same time, secretly working on an armistice proposal. He played both roles with routine determination, including taking the arguments back to Hitler in meetings and memoranda, the last of which was sent on 15 July. Two days later he was diligently rushing hither and thither across the Normandy countryside in his efforts to improve the German troops' deployment when, towards the end of the afternoon, returning from a meeting with Sepp Dietrich, his car was strafed by an Allied aircraft as it sped between Livarot and Vimoutiers. This removed him from the fast-developing plans of the conspirators, but their schemes did not need their preferred leader to be present.

Rommel was thus oblivious of the mysterious moves at a meeting in Hitler's headquarters at Rastenburg on 20 July when Colonel Count von Stauffenberg left a suitcase in the temporary building in which Hitler was to speak. The bomb exploded but the thin construction of the room dissipated the force and only limited injuries were inflicted. The devastation stimulated an announcement that Hitler had been killed only for him to emerge as an 'unscathed hero of an assassination attempt'. Immediately the hunt began for the many suspects and, under pressure of interrogation, several of them implicated Rommel.

The injuries he had suffered should have killed the Swabian, but, with typical inner resolve, he was receiving visitors at the hospital just one week after the incident, even persuading a visitor to take a photograph of him 'from his good side' in order to show the British that 'they haven't managed to kill me yet'. He was told of the assassination attempt and is reported to have told Admiral Ruge that it was 'altogether the wrong way to go about it.'[19] Ruge is said to have sought to get Rommel out of the country, such was the purge of possible conspirators already underway, but he could not get the loyal German to agree and by mid-August the German hero was back at his home in Herrlingen. His son was relieved of his duties at a gun site at Ulm in order to help his father's convalescence.

Aware that many of those who were more or less implicated in the Bomb Plot – including his good friend and fellow Württemberger, Lieutenant-General Hans Speidel – were being rounded up and von Kluge had committed suicide, Rommel was mindful that he might receive 'visitors' while he was recovering, but remained confident that his role had been so innocuous that Hitler could only accuse him of being a dissenter, for he had done his best in Normandy and was not supportive of the assassination attempt; in the world of Erwin Rommel opposite arguments were listened to and were not cause for imprisonment or worse. But the death of von Kluge was significant to him as he was, like Rommel, more non- than anti-Nazi and only got involved in direct opposition moves once he had heard the reports that Hitler was dead.

By September, when he received a visit from Strölin, he was armed with a pistol and told his friend that suspicious people had been seen in the area and that he was afraid only of Russians and Germans. A few days later he was unwisely stirred into vitriolic condemnation of Hitler during a visit by a local Party boss whose ability to report such an exchange to Berlin is undeniable but unproved. On 1 October he even wrote to Hitler complaining that he could not understand what could have led to Speidel's arrest and, by doing so, would have both annoyed the leader and effectively put himself in greater danger still.

As his health improved he began to travel short distances for further treatment and now a request came for him to visit Berlin on 10 October. Rommel telephoned Berlin to verify the reason for the meeting and was told it was to consider his future employment, but, still ill and surely not likely to have his state improved by such a journey, he replied that his doctor, Professor Albrecht, would not give permission for the trip. Admiral Ruge came to stay with Rommel on 11 October and found the Field Marshal convinced that if he travelled unguarded to Berlin he would not get there alive.

Two days later Rommel was told to expect a visit the following day from Generals Wilhelm Burgdorf and Ernst Maisel, the latter being from the Personnel branch. Before the visitors arrived, Rommel went for a walk with his son, Manfred, during which the conversation moved between what Rommel expected of the meeting and what he hoped his son's future might hold; he urged upon him a career as a doctor rather than a soldier.

The meeting with the Generals lasted almost an hour and was polite and calm. The visitors then left the room but waited outside while Rommel explained to his tearful wife that he had had it explained to him that the bomb plotters had implicated him in their plan, that a paper had been found showing Rommel as President of the Reich, and the Führer offered him two choices, trial by a people's court during which his reputation would be destroyed, and all the consequences that would have for his family, or suicide and a state funeral. He said the visitors had brought the poison and told him it would be effective within seconds. When his wife pleaded with him to accept the trial he replied by saying that it was no real option as he believed he would be killed on the way to Berlin.

The man who had fought with heroic bravery for his country in two wars and had inspired thousands of his fellow countrymen on the battlefield ordered his wife and son to remain silent so that Hitler would be given no cause to renege on his undertaking. He left with the generals and a few minutes later a telephone call confirmed his death. Even before the state funeral on 18 October, the family received dreadfully formal and wretched letters of sympathy from Hitler, Goebbels and Göring among others.

Having cheated death in his nation's two most awesome wars, Erwin Rommel died by his own hand at the instigation of the leader he had come to despise. That he sought to save his wife and son from the pain a public trial would have brought them – had it got that far – was testament to the man's humanity, a quality he showed in the heat of battle as well as in his life.

Erwin Rommel brought a daring and élan to the darkness of war; it earned him the respect of friend and foe alike. He did not possess every talent his military tutors might have sought to instil, but, by their efforts and his own, he made more of himself than anyone could have expected, and there is no better praise. He was unique and had genius and it is remarkable that in the news-driven days since his time no military leader has earned such hero-worship and professional admiration.

Rommel's state funeral, October 1944, the true circumstances of his death concealed from the German people.

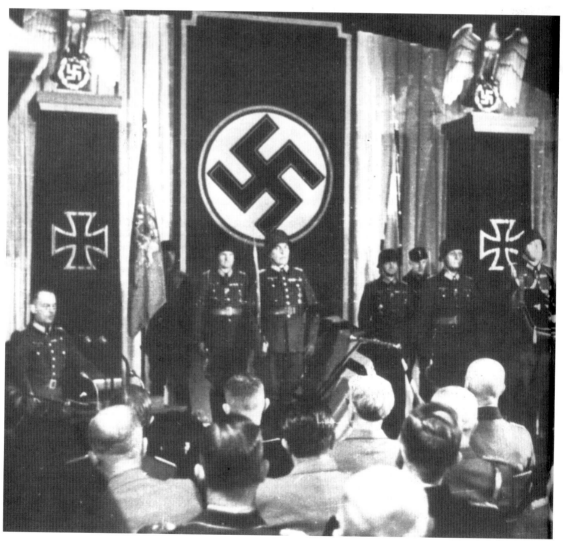